Thriving With Anxiety

Anxiety and Phobias

By

Danae Long

Copyright

All rights reserved. No part of this publication may be reproduced, distributed, or transmitted in any form or by any means, including photocopying, recording, or other electronic or mechanical methods, without the prior written permission of the publisher, except in the case of brief quotations embodied in critical reviews and certain other non-commercial uses permitted by copyright law.

Disclaimer

Thriving with Anxiety by Danae Long is an inspirational guide based on personal thoughts and experiences. This book should not be used in place of professional counsel. Readers are strongly advised to seek the advice of experienced healthcare specialists. The author and publisher accept no responsibility for any consequences resulting from the use of the material in this book.

About The Author

 **Danae Long** is an outspoken supporter of mental health and well-being. Danae brings a unique blend of academic understanding and lived experience to her writing, with a degree in psychology and a personal journey of conquering anxiety. Her purpose is to help people thrive in the face of anxiety by providing practical techniques and a sympathetic perspective. Danae enjoys nature hikes, reading, and establishing a supportive network for individuals on similar journeys when she is not involved in the realm of mental health activism. Danae's heartfelt contribution to the conversation around mental health is **Thriving**

with Anxiety, which offers direction and encouragement to individuals seeking to live happy lives despite the presence of anxiety. Danae's work attempts to dispel stigma, create understanding, and instill hope in the hearts of her readers.

Quick Guide

Do You Want To Know About Anxiety?
- Open To Chapter 1&2

Want To Understand Phobias?
- Open To Page 44

Want To Recognize Triggers?
- Open To page 67

Want to Know About Breathing and Relaxation Techniques
- Open to Page 76

Want To Know About Meditation and Mindfulness
- Open To Page 84

Want To Know How to Overcome Social Anxiety
- Open To Chapter 5

Mental Health Support Helplines And Hotlines

- Open To Page 248

But If You are Really Curious To Know More On How To Deal With Anxiety and Phobias Then Exercise Patient and Read Through.

Table of Content

Thriving With Anxiety and Phobias

INTRODUCTION

Why This Book Is Important

Anxiety and phobias are two frequent mental health issues that millions of individuals suffer from on a daily basis. Fear, dread, and discomfort can be incapacitating, affecting many aspects of life, from personal connections to career possibilities. If you or someone you know has ever struggled with anxiety or phobias, you're probably aware of how powerful they can be. Because of the importance of these issues, I chose to create this book in order to shed light on them and provide guidance and assistance to those in need.

In this article, "Why This Book Matters," we will look at why this self-help book was created and what you may expect to gain from it.

1. Raising Awareness and Reducing Stigma: One of the key reasons this book is important is the urgent need to promote awareness and decrease the stigma associated with anxiety and phobias. Unfortunately, many people still regard mental health issues as a sign of weakness or a deficiency in character.

This stigma frequently hinders people from obtaining the care they require. We hope to shift the debate towards empathy and understanding by discussing these concerns openly and honestly. Recognizing the frequency of anxiety and phobias might help people realize they are not alone in their challenges and that seeking help and support is acceptable.

2. Providing Information and Education: Anxiety and phobias can be complex and difficult to understand, both for those who suffer from them and for those who care for them. This book is intended to provide a comprehensive and easily accessible source of information about these illnesses. It defines anxiety and phobias, their different manifestations, the symptoms linked to them, and how they might affect one's life. The first step towards effective management and rehabilitation is to understand the underlying causes and manifestations of anxiety and phobias. We hope that by offering this information, readers will be able to take charge of their mental health.

3. Providing Practical Advice and Strategies: Anxiety and phobias do not have to be insurmountable. Individuals can learn to control their symptoms and live full lives with the correct tools and tactics. This book provides practical advice and evidence-based solutions for dealing with anxiety and phobias. There is a variety of actionable information available, ranging from relaxation techniques and self-help activities to insights from therapy and personal success stories. Furthermore, the book addresses specific types of anxiety and phobias, such as social anxiety and panic attacks, with individually customized approaches for each. Readers will discover how to face their anxieties, build resilience, and regain control of their lives.

4. Encouraging a Holistic Approach: Mental health is more than just treating symptoms; it is also about nurturing general well-being. This book provides a comprehensive approach to mental health by delving into the relationship between lifestyle, self-care, and mental health. It dives into the significance of a well-balanced diet, regular exercise, adequate relaxation, and stress management as components of a comprehensive mental health strategy. The goal is to inspire readers to develop habits and practices that promote their emotional and mental well-being, in addition to addressing their anxieties and phobias.

5. Motivating hope and resilience: The theme of optimism and resilience is perhaps one of the most important components of this book. Throughout its pages, you will find accounts of people who have overcome anxiety and phobias. These personal stories are both an inspiration and a testament to the human ability for growth and transformation. We hope that by sharing these tales, we will encourage hope in readers who are feeling overwhelmed by their own issues. The message is clear: healing is possible, and there is hope for a better future.

6. Encouraging Professional Assistance: While this book contains a plethora of information and self-help tactics, it is critical to emphasize the need to obtain professional assistance when necessary. The intensity of anxiety and phobias varies, and not everyone can overcome them alone through self-help strategies. Recognizing when it's time to see a therapist or psychiatrist is a critical step in the rehabilitation process. This book acts as a guide to help people understand their condition and provides advice on how to get the most out of therapy and medication when they are needed.

7. Creating a Friendly Community: We understand that overcoming anxiety and phobias is not a single endeavor. It frequently entails the assistance of loved ones, friends, and mental health specialists. We believe that this book will help readers develop a sense of community. You are not alone in your battle, and you can connect with others who are on similar routes by reading and sharing your stories. A supporting community's cumulative strength can be a fantastic source of encouragement and drive.

This book is essential because it covers a critical and frequently misunderstood component of human existence: mental health. Anxiety and phobias are common, and their consequences can be severe. This book attempts to empower individuals to successfully navigate their mental health difficulties by providing education, guidance, and inspiration. Remember that your well-being is paramount, and there is assistance available. This book is a resource, a companion, and a guide to understanding, managing, and ultimately overcoming anxiety and phobias. It is important because your mental health is important.

Who This Book Is For

As I continue on this path to provide insights and help to those suffering from anxiety and phobias, it's critical to understand who this book's intended audience is. "Who This Book Is For" is a guide to help you choose whether the information included within these pages is a relevant and valuable resource for your specific situation.

1. People Suffering From Anxiety and Phobias

This book is primarily intended for people who are currently suffering from anxiety disorders or phobias, or who suspect they may be. If you are dealing with chronic, upsetting worries, fears, or panic attacks, this book is intended to provide you with guidance, hope, and practical solutions for dealing with and overcoming these issues.

2. Supporters and Loved Ones

Anxiety and phobias affect more than just the people who suffer from them; they also have a huge impact on their loved ones. This book is also for you if you are a family member, friend, or partner of someone who is suffering from anxiety or phobias. It will assist you in gaining a better understanding of these disorders as well as insights into how to provide support and encouragement.

3. Those Attempting to Understand Mental Health

Even if you do not suffer from anxiety or phobias, understanding mental health is critical to our overall well-being. Anyone interested in understanding the intricacies of the human mind and emotions may find this book useful. You can learn about how mental health issues manifest and how to deal with them.

4. Professionals in Mental Health

This book is also useful for mental health professionals such as therapists, counselors, and psychologists. While the primary focus is on offering help to people suffering from anxiety and phobias, the book also provides an overview of evidence-based treatments and approaches that professionals can use in their practice. It could be a useful resource for staying current on the latest techniques for treating these illnesses.

5. Individuals Interested in Self-Help and Personal Development

If you are interested in personal growth and self-help, this book can be a beneficial addition to your library. Whether or not you suffer from anxiety or phobias, the ideas and activities on these pages can help you on your personal growth journey. Resilience, self-compassion, and holistic well-being are principles that can be applied to many aspects of life.

6. Anyone Looking For Motivation and Hope

Finally, this book is for everyone looking for motivation and optimism. You will read stories about people who overcame seemingly insurmountable obstacles in these chapters. Their stories serve as beacons of hope, demonstrating that healing is possible and that better days are ahead. Even if you are not personally impacted by anxiety or phobias, these stories can motivate you to overcome your own problems and help others around you.

This book is a thorough handbook written with sensitivity and competence for a wide and diverse audience. Whether you are dealing with anxiety or phobias, supporting someone who is, or simply seeking knowledge and inspiration, these pages have something for you. Our unifying goal is to enhance comprehension, resilience, and healing in the face of these prevalent yet difficult mental health disorders. Remember that you are not alone on your journey, and this book offers assistance to anyone in need, no matter where you are on your route to greater mental health.

How to Use This Book

You may be wondering how to make the most of the book now that you have it in your hands. We're here to show you how to use this book successfully to understand, manage, and eventually overcome the difficulties of anxiety and phobias.

1. Begin with an introduction: The preface welcomes you to the universe of this novel. It's where you'll learn why this book is important and who it's for. Understanding the book's purpose and target audience can assist you in connecting with its content and goals. Take a moment to consider how this book fits your needs and expectations.

2. Go at Your Own Pace When Reading: When it comes to self-help, there is no haste.

This book is meant to be read at your own speed. Each chapter is intended to be a stand-alone resource, allowing you to delve into the areas that are most interesting to you. If a section does not apply to your situation, you may skip it and return later if necessary.

3.   Self-Reflection   and   Evaluation: Self-assessment exercises and questions are sprinkled throughout the text. These are meant to assist you in reflecting on your experiences, symptoms, and triggers. Take your time and do these activities honestly and thoughtfully. They will give you significant insight into your specific circumstances.

4. Implementable Strategies: One of this book's main merits is its emphasis on actionable techniques. As you go through the chapters on anxiety management, coping methods, and resilience building, keep in mind that these are not theoretical concepts. They are tools that must be put to use. Experiment with the tasks, strategies, and suggestions provided. Experiment with what works best for you and customize it to your own situation.

5. Relate To Personal Experiences: Personal accounts of people who overcame anxiety and phobias are sprinkled throughout the book. These stories provide a strong source of inspiration and optimism. As you read them, think about how you can relate to these people's hardships and successes. Recognize that their experiences are similar to yours and that they are living proof that recovery is possible.

6. Seek Professional Assistance When Necessary: While this book contains a plethora of self-help ideas, it is critical to Recognize when professional assistance is required.

Consider getting the help of a mental health professional if your anxiety or phobias are severe or severely interfering with your life. This book can help you in your therapeutic journey, but it is not a replacement for personalized care.

7. Make Contact With A Helpful Community: Anxiety and phobias can be very isolating, but you are not alone. This book promotes a sense of belonging. Engage with the content, offer your perspectives, and connect with others who are dealing with similar issues. You can seek help from friends, relatives, or support groups who understand your situation.

8. Exercise self-compassion: Above all, while you read through this book, practice self-compassion. Be patient and nice to yourself. Healing is a journey that frequently includes setbacks and hardships. Accept your progress, no matter how insignificant it may appear, and remember that you have the strength to overcome your challenges.

This self-help book is a diverse and compassionate resource that will aid you on your path to mental well-being. Use it as a guide, inspiration, and partner on your healing journey. Your mental health is important, and this book is here to assist you as you negotiate the complexity of anxiety and phobias. Accept its substance, implement its tactics, and keep in mind that rehabilitation is not only attainable but also within your grasp.

CHAPTER 1

Understanding Anxiety and Phobias

Anxiety and phobias are frequent experiences that many people have at some point in their lives. They are a part of the human condition, and Recognizing them can help us better manage our mental health. We will explain the complicated concepts of anxiety and phobias in this essay so that you can grasp what they are and how they might affect our lives.

Anxiety: The Universal Emotion

Anxiety is something that we all encounter sometimes. It is a basic human feeling that is frequently referred to as the body's natural response to stress. Anxiety is essentially your body's way of warning you of prospective hazards or dangers. It's similar to a built-in alarm system. Assume you're going through a forest when you hear a rustle in the bushes. Your heart rate increases, your muscles strain, and your thinking sharpens. These physical and psychological responses are your body's method of preparing you to respond to a potential attack. This is a normal and healthy sort of anxiety, also known as "fight or flight."

Anxiety might emerge as concern, nervousness, or unease in everyday life. It's the sensation you get before a large presentation, an important exam, or when confronted with an unfamiliar situation. This is a typical reaction to life's obstacles, and it may actually be motivating, driving you to prepare and perform at your best.

Anxiety, on the other hand, might interfere with your daily life if it becomes extreme, chronic, or uncontrollable. It may be difficult for you to concentrate, relax, or even sleep. This is the point at which anxiety transitions from a beneficial emotion to a problem that requires care.

Phobias: Intense Fears of Certain Things.

In contrast, phobias are a more particular and powerful sort of anxiety. A phobia is an intense and illogical fear of a specific thing, place, or species. While certain anxieties are normal, such as being terrified of spiders or heights, phobias carry these worries to an extreme. When a person faces the object of their fear, they frequently experience tremendous panic or anxiety. For example, someone who is afraid of flying may experience crushing fear and anxiety just thinking about boarding an airplane. This dread can be so great that it causes avoidance behaviors, which cause major disturbances in daily living.

Phobias are Grouped Into Several Categories:

Specific Fears: These are phobias of specific objects or circumstances, such as spiders, needles, or flying.

Social Anxiety Disorder (SAD): Is a dread of social events and interactions in which people are afraid of being evaluated, embarrassed, or humiliated in public.

Agoraphobia: Is the fear of being in situations or places where escape is difficult, such as crowded areas or open spaces.

Panic Disorder: Although not necessarily considered a phobia, panic disorder is characterized by unexpected and recurring panic attacks. These attacks can be accompanied by strong physical symptoms such as a racing heart, perspiration, and a sense of being out of control.

The Relationship Between Anxiety and Phobias

So, what is the link between anxiety and phobias?

It is critical to Recognize that all phobias are a type of anxiety illness. They are distinct types of anxiety characterized by acute, unreasonable worries about specific things or circumstances. Someone with social anxiety disorder, for example, has significant anxiety in social situations, which is a type of anxiety disorder. Similarly, someone who has a fear of heights (acrophobia) has a specific phobia tied to a specific object or event. Anxiety lies at the heart of both of these feelings. It is the emotion that causes the great fear and the bodily and emotional responses that accompany it. This is why, in the realm of mental health, phobias are frequently treated as a subtype of anxiety disorders.

When Anxiety and Phobias Becomes a Problem

While anxiety and phobias are natural parts of life, they can be harmful if they:

Interfere with Day-to-Day Life: Anxiety and phobias become an issue when they interfere with your ability to work, study, maintain relationships, or enjoy ordinary activities.

Causes Physical Symptoms: Excessive anxiety can cause physical symptoms such as racing hearts, perspiration, trembling, and stomach troubles, making it difficult to function.

Persist Over Time: If your anxiety or fear persists over a lengthy period of time, it may be a sign of an anxiety disorder that requires treatment.

Result in Avoidance: Avoiding situations or items out of dread is a common symptom of a phobia. This avoidance has the potential to limit your life experience.

Management and Treatment

The good news is that anxiety and phobias can be treated. There are numerous therapeutic techniques and self-help strategies available to assist individuals in managing and overcoming these issues. If you or someone you love is suffering from anxiety or a phobia, seeking help from a mental health expert is an important step towards recovering control of your life.

Anxiety is a normal reaction to stress and prospective threats, whereas phobias are extreme, illogical dreads of certain objects or situations. Both are natural parts of the human experience, but when they become excessive or disruptive, they may indicate anxiety disorders that require treatment. Understanding these emotions and their impact is the first step towards good management.

Types of Anxiety Disorder

Each is distinguished by its symptoms and triggers. Here is a list of some of the most prevalent anxiety disorders, along with brief descriptions of each: **Generalized Anxiety Disorder (GAD):** This is characterized by excessive worry and anxiety about a wide range of everyday concerns, frequently with no apparent cause or justification. Physical signs of GAD include muscle tension, restlessness, and difficulty concentrating.

Panic disorder: This involves sudden and strong panic attacks, as well as physical symptoms such as a racing heart, shortness of breath, and perspiration. People may develop a fear of experiencing more panic attacks.

Social Anxiety Disorder (Social Phobia): People with social anxiety experience extreme anxiety and self-consciousness in social situations. They frequently avoid social engagements because they are afraid of being judged, humiliated, or embarrassed in front of others.

Specific Phobias: This kind of phobias are extreme and unreasonable dreads of specific items, circumstances, or creatures. Arachnophobia (fear of spiders) and acrophobia (fear of heights) are two common examples.

Agoraphobia: This is the fear of being in situations or locations where exit would be difficult or embarrassing. This can result in avoiding busy areas, public transit, or open spaces.

Separation Anxiety Disorder: Separation anxiety disorder is most common among children, but it can last into adulthood. Excessive anxiety about being away from a loved one, such as a parent, caregiver, or partner, is involved.

Selective mutism: is a childhood anxiety problem in which a child does not speak in certain social contexts despite speaking in others. This is related to significant social anxiety rather than a lack of language skills.

Obsessive-Compulsive Disorder (OCD): OCD is characterized by intrusive and persistent thoughts (obsessions) and repetitive behaviors or mental acts (compulsions) aimed at alleviating the misery produced by the obsessions. Fears of contamination or damage are common obsessions, while repeated hand washing or checking are common compulsions.

Post-terrible stress disorder (PTSD): PTSD can develop as a result of witnessing or experiencing a terrible event. It is distinguished by symptoms such as flashbacks, nightmares, acute anxiety, and avoidance of the traumatic event.

Body Dysmorphic Disorder (BDD): BDD is characterized by an intense emphasis on perceived defects in physical appearance that others may not notice. Individuals suffering from BDD engage in obsessive behaviors to relieve their anxiety, such as excessive grooming or seeking reassurance.

Illness Anxiety Disorder (Hypochondriasis): People with illness anxiety disorder are too concerned about getting a major illness, even if there is no medical proof to back up their anxieties.

They may seek medical reassurance on a regular basis and engage in health-related behaviors, such as frequent clinic visits. Each of these anxiety disorders has its own set of symptoms and causes, and their severity might vary. If you or someone you love is experiencing signs of an anxiety disorder, it is critical to seek professional help since effective treatment options, such as therapy and medication, are available to help manage and alleviate the symptoms.

Understanding Common Phobias

Certain phobias, also known as common phobias, are acute and illogical dreads of certain items, situations, or creatures. These worries can cause severe anxiety, even to the point of producing panic attacks. While some anxieties are acceptable, typical phobias carry these fears to an extreme, greatly affecting an individual's everyday life.

Some of The Most Frequent Phobias Are As Follows:

Arachnophobia (Fear of Spiders): One of the most well-known phobias is arachnophobia. Those who have this fear may suffer tremendous anxiety and avoid situations where spiders may be present. Fear frequently extends to any spider, regardless of size or harmlessness.

Acrophobia (Fear of Heights): Acrophobic people experience great fear and anxiety when they are exposed to heights, even when they are safe. This anxiety might cause people to avoid big buildings, bridges, and even escalators.

Claustrophobia (Dread of Confined Spaces): Claustrophobia is the dread of being in enclosed or restricted spaces, such as lifts, tunnels or crowded rooms. Individuals suffering from this phobia may experience panic attacks in such settings.

Agoraphobia (Fear of Open or Crowded Spaces): Agoraphobia is characterized by a fear of being in settings or locations where escape would be difficult or embarrassing. This can result in avoiding busy areas, public transit, or open spaces.

Ophidiophobia (Snake Fear): Ophidiophobia is a widespread fear of snakes. Those who suffer with this phobia may experience great anxiety or fear when they come into contact with these reptiles, even if they offer no threat.

Aviophobia (Fear of Flying): People who have aviophobia experience intense anxiety and fear when flying in planes. This anxiety might cause people to avoid flying, restricting their personal and professional options.

Common phobias can have a substantial influence on a person's quality of life, including avoidance behaviors, discomfort, and, in some cases, physical symptoms such as high heart rate, perspiration, and trembling. These phobias frequently emerge during childhood or adolescence and, if untreated, can last into adulthood.

Common phobias, thankfully, are curable. Cognitive-behavioral therapy (CBT) is a popular and successful method for dealing with phobias. Exposure therapy, a kind of CBT, involves progressively and securely exposing people to the object or circumstance that they are afraid of, allowing them to desensitize and diminish their anxiety reaction.

In Some Circumstances, Medication May Be Explored.

Understanding common phobias and obtaining professional help when necessary can enable people to confront their fears, reclaim control of their life, and find relief from the overwhelming anxiety associated with these illogical worries.

Anxiety and Phobias and Their Effects In Our Life

While anxiety and phobias are prevalent, they can have substantial and far-reaching repercussions on a person's life. These are not just passing concerns or fears; they are frequently persistent, strong, and disruptive. Understanding how anxiety and phobias affect your life is critical for finding appropriate treatment and effectively managing their impact.

1. Interfering With Daily Operations:

Anxiety and phobias can interfere with your daily life in a variety of ways. Excessive anxiety, fear, or panic might make it difficult to focus on duties at home or at work. You may struggle to concentrate, make decisions, or perform to your full ability.

2. Interfering with Social Relationships:

Social anxiety and specific phobias can make it difficult to establish good relationships. You may avoid social engagements or situations that cause anxiety, resulting to feelings of isolation and loneliness. Personal, familial, and professional connections may be strained as a result.

Phobia-related avoidance behaviors, such as avoiding airplanes owing to aviophobia or avoiding crowded locations due to agoraphobia, might limit your professional options. Your unwillingness to participate in certain professional activities may impede your progress and achievement.

4. Health Consequences:

Living with chronic anxiety can have a negative impact on your physical health. It can cause high blood pressure, gastrointestinal issues, and an increased risk of cardiovascular disease.

Anxiety's continual fight-or-flight response can fatigue the body over time.

5. Sleep Disorders:

Anxiety and phobias frequently cause sleep problems such as sleeplessness or nightmares. Inadequate sleep can aggravate anxiety and have a negative influence on your entire health and well-being.

6. Avoidance behaviors:

People who have phobias typically go to considerable lengths to avoid events, objects, or locations that make them anxious. As avoidance behaviors limit one's experiences and chances, this might lead to a shrinking world.

7. Procrastination and Avoidance:

Anxiety can lead to procrastination because you may postpone duties to escape the anxiety that comes with them. This can reduce your productivity and increase your stress.

8. Physical Symptoms:

Anxiety and phobias can emerge physically, with symptoms such as racing heart, perspiration, shaking, and shortness of breath. These physical sensations might be upsetting and have an influence on your general well-being.

9. Economic Consequences:

Phobias and anxiety can have a financial impact. If your anxieties cause you to miss work, seek medical treatment, or engage in avoidance behaviors that necessitate financial resources, your financial stability may suffer.

10. Quality of Life:

Anxiety and phobias have a broad impact on your overall quality of life. These diseases have the potential to deprive you of the satisfaction and fulfillment that comes from living a balanced, healthy, and well-rounded life. Your capacity to follow your passions, participate in hobbies, and simply enjoy everyday situations can be severely hampered.

It's critical to understand that anxiety and phobias can be treated. Seeking the assistance of a mental health expert can provide useful ways for dealing with these issues and regaining control of your life. Therapy, medicine, self-help strategies, or a mix of these treatments may be used as treatment alternatives.

Understanding the life-altering effects of anxiety and phobias is the first step towards addressing and managing these diseases. It is possible to lessen the impact of anxiety and phobias and improve your general well-being with the correct help and tactics.

CHAPTER 2

Recognizing Your Anxiety and Phobias

SIGNS AND SYMPTOMS

Anxiety symptoms include:

Excessive Worry: is defined as persistent, uncontrollable, and excessive worrying over numerous elements of one's life, frequently with no apparent explanation.

Restlessness: The sensation of being on edge, restless, or unable to relax. Fidgeting, pacing, or an inability to sit still may be symptoms.

Muscle Tension: Anxiety-related physical symptoms include muscle stiffness, tension headaches, and jaw clenching.

Fatigue: Feeling weary all the time, even after getting enough sleep, because anxiety can be mentally and physically exhausting.

Irritability: The ability to become easily angry, agitated, or to have a short temper. Small stimuli might elicit a strong reaction.

Sleep Disturbance: Insomnia, frequent waking, or severe dreams caused by racing thoughts or worry.

Difficulty Concentration: Inability to focus, make decisions, or think clearly owing to racing thoughts and anxiety-related mental preoccupation.

Physical Symptoms: This include racing heart, shortness of breath, shaking, sweating, and nausea.

Symptoms of Phobia:

Intense terror: An instantaneous, intense, and unreasonable terror when exposed to the phobia's item or circumstance.

Panic Attacks: In severe circumstances, the phobic environment or object can cause panic attacks, which are characterized by symptoms including a racing heart, perspiration, trembling, and a sensation of impending doom.

Avoidance Behavior: Individuals with phobias may go to great lengths to avoid situations or objects that trigger their fears, limiting their experiences and opportunities.

Overwhelming Anxiety: Phobia-related anxiety can be overwhelming, causing distress and occasionally causing physical symptoms such as heart palpitations or nausea.

Anticipatory Anxiety: Fear of the future exposure can cause anxiety long before experiencing the phobic object or situation.

Impact on Daily Life: Phobias can have a considerable influence on daily life, restricting personal and professional chances and generating severe distress.

It is vital to note that the severity of anxiety and phobia symptoms might vary. While some people have minor or infrequent symptoms, others have more strong and chronic types of anxiety or phobias that interfere with their everyday life.

If you or someone you know is experiencing these symptoms to the point where they are interfering with everyday functioning and well-being, it is strongly advised that you get professional help. To control anxiety and phobias and enhance overall quality of life, mental health specialists can provide effective treatment choices such as therapy, medication, and self-help strategies.

Exercises in Self-Assessment

It's easy to get caught up in the rush and bustle of our fast-paced life and lose sight of our personal progress and fulfillment. This is when self-assessment exercises come into play. These activities are useful tools for pausing, reflecting, and gaining a better understanding of ourselves, our objectives, and our aspirations. In this articleLet's look at the importance of self-assessment activities and how they may be used to unlock your potential and lead you to personal growth and fulfillment .

What I Mean By Self-Assessment Exercises?
Self-assessment exercises are planned activities or procedures that help people to review different elements of their lives, such as their strengths, shortcomings, values, objectives, and

emotions. These activities serve as a foundation for introspection and self-discovery, assisting you in discovering who you are, what you desire, and how to get there. Questionnaires, diary prompts, examinations, and organized reflections are examples of these exercises. They are intended to help you connect with your ideas and feelings more deeply, helping you to make more informed decisions and perform more purposeful actions.

Why Self-Assessment Exercises Are Important

Self-Assessment activities are important since they serve as a guidepost for your life journey. Here's why they're so useful:

1. Self-Discovery: Self-Assessment tasks help you find hidden aspects of your personality, values, and desires. They assist you in exploring your strengths and shortcomings, presenting a complete picture of who you are. This self-discovery serves as the foundation for personal development and transformation.

2. Goal Clarity: Self-assessment activities help you develop clear and meaningful goals by reflecting on your passions, interests, and aspirations. You develop a greater knowledge of what you want to accomplish and the procedures necessary to achieve your goals.

3. Better Decision-Making: Making educated judgements is critical to personal and professional success. Self-assessment activities provide the knowledge needed to make choices that are consistent with your beliefs and priorities, resulting in improved outcomes.

4. Increased Self-Awareness: Emotional intelligence and self-management are both built on self-awareness. You can discover your emotions, reactions, and triggers through self-assessment, allowing you to respond more intelligently to life's problems.

5. Personal Development: Self-Assessment is an important aspect of personal development. It assists you in establishing a clear direction for your development and in developing a framework for continuous improvement.

Different Types of Self-Assessment Exercises

Self-assessment tasks cover a wide range of topics and cater to numerous parts of your life and personal growth. Here are some examples of frequent self-assessment exercises:

1. Assessment of Strengths and Weaknesses: This exercise allows you to discover your strengths and places for improvement. Knowing your talents allows you to capitalize on them, while accepting your flaws allows you to progress.

2. Values Assessment: Values are the guiding principles in your life. This exercise will assist you in identifying your values, which will be helpful in making decisions and developing meaningful goals.

3. Goal Setting and Planning: Develop a vision for your future by establishing short-term and long-term objectives. Outline the measures required to realize them, turning your dreams into actionable strategies.

4. Emotional Intelligence Evaluation: Evaluate your emotional intelligence by reflecting on your emotional reactions and interactions with others. Recognizing and controlling emotions is critical for both personal and professional success.

5. Life Wheel Assessment: The life wheel exercise categorizes your life by work, health, relationships, and personal growth. This tool assists you in evaluating your degree of satisfaction in each area, emphasizing areas that need to be addressed.

6. Journaling and Reflection: Keeping a journal and reflecting on a regular basis is an ongoing Self-Assessment practice. Write down your thoughts, experiences, and feelings, and then go back over them to obtain new insights throughout time.

How to Maximize Self-Assessment Exercises

Consider the following suggestions for properly utilizing the potential of self-assessment exercises:

1. Establish a Routine:

Incorporate Self-Assessment into your daily, weekly, or monthly routine. Consistency is essential for developing significant insights over time.

2. Be Honest with Yourself: True Self-Assessment necessitates honesty. Be open to confronting your own strengths and weaknesses without prejudice.

3. Establish Specific Goals: Using self-assessment exercises, clearly state the goals you wish to achieve. A purpose will provide your Self-Assessment a feeling of direction.

4. Seek Feedback: Seek feedback from reliable friends, family members, or mentors. Their viewpoints can provide extra insights into your Self-Assessment .

5. Take Action: Self-Assessment should be followed by action. Implement ways to move forward once you've identified areas for improvement or set goals.

6. Adapt and Evolve: Your self-assessment tasks should evolve with you as you grow and change. Make changes to reflect your changing values, priorities, and ambitions.

Also, keep in mind that Self-Assessment tasks are more than just exercises in introspection; they are dynamic tools for personal progress and fulfillment. You can construct a path to a more purposeful and satisfying life by evaluating your talents, limitations, values, and objectives. Accept Self-Assessment as a continuing voyage of self-discovery, and allow it to take you to the finest version of yourself. Remember that the ability to grow and evolve is within you, waiting to be released through the practice of Self-Assessment .

Trigger Recognition

Life can be a complicated web of events, emotions, and reactions. We can find ourselves caught in the clutches of overwhelming emotions without warning at times. These moments are frequently prompted by specific events or circumstances, and Recognizing and understanding these triggers is an important step towards emotional well-being. Let's look at the concept of triggers, their importance, and effective methods for identifying them.

What Exactly Are Triggers?

External or internal stimuli that cause significant emotional reactions or responses are referred to as triggers. Events, settings, phrases, smells, memories, or even bodily sensations can all be examples. Triggers frequently cause anguish, anxiety, wrath, sadness, or fear. While some triggers are obvious, others may be hidden beneath the surface and require introspection and self-awareness to detect.

The Importance of Trigger Recognition

Recognizing and comprehending triggers is critical for a number of reasons:

Emotional Regulation: Recognizing triggers allows you to anticipate and moderate emotional reactions. This, in turn, gives you the ability to control your emotions and avoid overreacting.

Conflict Resolution: Recognizing triggers in relationships and interpersonal interactions allows you to avoid or handle disputes more effectively. It can also encourage compassionate communication.

Self-Awareness: Recognizing triggers increases your self-awareness. It illuminates your emotional patterns and provides useful insights into your inner world.

Healing and Development: Identifying triggers is a critical step in recovering from prior traumas or unresolved difficulties. It enables you to face and process the emotions linked with these triggers.

Improved Decision-Making: Knowing your emotional triggers might help you make better decisions and avoid impulsive reactions.

Triggers of Common Interest

Triggers differ significantly from person to person, but some prevalent ones are as follows:

Trauma Triggers: Events or circumstances that remind a person of a traumatic experience might elicit strong emotional reactions. These triggers can be difficult to Recognize and handle.

Triggers in Relationships: Interactions with specific people or situations within relationships can be major triggers. They can make you feel insecure, angry, or jealous.

Environmental Triggers: Sensory stimulation, such as specific smells or locations, can elicit emotional responses. The aroma of a specific perfume, for example, may recall memories and feelings.

Work-Related Triggers: Work-related stressors such as deadlines, performance assessments, or confrontations with coworkers can cause anxiety or dissatisfaction.

Negative Self-Talk: Triggers can be your internal speech and mental patterns. Self-criticism and negative self-talk can lead to feelings of inadequacy and self-doubt.

Triggers of Loss and loss: Anniversaries, holidays, or specific reminders of a lost loved one might cause loss and melancholy.

Trigger Identification Techniques

Mindfulness: Mindfulness is the focused, nonjudgmental attention to the present moment. This increased awareness can assist you in identifying triggers when they occur.

Journaling: Recording your thoughts, emotions, and the events or situations around your triggers in a journal can provide significant insights over time.

Therapy: Professional therapy or counseling can provide a safe place to explore and identify triggers, especially if they are associated with trauma or complex emotions.

Self-Reflection: Self-reflection on a regular basis might reveal patterns and themes in your emotional responses. Consider why some events or encounters affect you the way they do.

Feedback from Others: Reliable friends, relatives, or a therapist can offer an outside viewpoint on your triggers, assisting you in identifying blind spots.

Sensations of the Body: When intense emotions arise, pay attention to your body's reactions. Clenched fists, a beating heart, or a lump in the throat are all signs of emotional triggers.

Trigger Management and Response

Identifying triggers is only the first step. The next step is to understand how to properly handle and respond to them:

Techniques for Deep Breathing and Relaxation: To keep calm and composed when a trigger appears, practice deep breathing and relaxation techniques.

Self-Care: Be gentle with yourself. Remember that everyone has triggers and that it's normal to feel vulnerable or emotional from time to time.

Grounding Exercises: Grounding exercises, such as focusing on your senses or using physical items, can help you stay in the present moment and lower the intensity of your emotional responses.

Seeking Help: If a trigger is very difficult, seeking help from friends, family, or a therapist can give a safe space for you to process your emotions.

Boundaries: Set clear boundaries in your relationships and at work to reduce your exposure to Recognized triggers.

Mindful Communication: Use mindful communication to successfully convey your needs and feelings in interpersonal conflicts.

Understanding and identifying triggers is an important step on your path to emotional well-being. Embrace the process of self-discovery and progress, and remember that identifying triggers is a powerful tool for emotional empowerment and personal development.

CHAPTER 3

Coping Strategies

TECHNIQUE FOR BREATHING AND RELAXATION

Breathing and relaxation techniques are extremely effective strategies for dealing with stress, anxiety, and emotional triggers. These techniques provide a realistic and approachable way to reclaim control of your mind and body, fostering calm, attention, and emotional resilience. Let's look at the significance of these approaches as well as a range of methods for mastering the art of relaxation and mindful breathing.

The Importance of Breathing and Relaxation Methods

Life is full of situations that might cause tension, anxiety, and emotional turmoil. Your body and mind can react with heightened tension and emotional responses to a job deadline, a difficult conversation, or a terrible memory. Breathing and relaxation exercises can help to address these emotions and restore homeostasis. Here's why these methods are important:

1. Stress Reduction: Deep breathing and relaxation techniques activate the body's relaxation response, which counteracts the stress response. This reduces stress hormones and promotes relaxation.

2. Emotional Regulation: These approaches allow you to better manage your emotions, reducing impulsive or overpowering reactions.

Staying grounded allows you to respond to difficult situations with greater calm.

3. Improved Focus: Mindful breathing and relaxation practices help you concentrate and think clearly. This sharpened attention can be beneficial in both personal and professional situations.

4. Improved Physical Health: Regular use of these strategies can enhance physical health by lowering blood pressure, improving digestion, and reducing muscle tension.

5. Better Sleep: By soothing your mind and alleviating tension, breathing and relaxation techniques help prepare your body for restful sleep, making it easier to fall and remain asleep.

Breathing and Relaxation Techniques: A Resilience Toolbox

To reap the benefits of mindful breathing and relaxation, there are several practical strategies you may implement into your everyday practice. Here are several popular approaches:

1. Diaphragmatic Deep Breathing:

Take calm, deep breaths from your diaphragm (the area right below your ribcage) with this technique. Deeply inhale through your nose, allowing your abdomen to expand, and slowly exhale through your mouth. Deep diaphragmatic breathing relieves tension and relaxes the neurological system.

2. Muscle Relaxation in Stages:

This technique is systematically tensing and then relaxing various muscle groups in your body. Begin at the bottom and work your way up, focusing on each muscle group as you go. This technique aids in the release of physical tension and the promotion of relaxation.

3. Visualization and guided imagery:

Close your eyes and visualize a quiet, serene setting. Consider yourself there, using all of your senses. Visualization can take you to a relaxing mental environment, decreasing tension and encouraging relaxation.

4. Meditation for Mindfulness:

Paying attention to the present moment without judgment is what mindfulness meditation entails. You can concentrate on your breathing, physical sensations, or the sounds around you. This practice promotes awareness and decreases stress and anxiety.

5. Breathing In a Box: Inhale for four counts, hold your breath for four counts, exhale for four counts, and then hold your breath for four more times. This easy practice aids in the regulation of your breathing and the relaxation of your nervous system.

6. Tai Chi and Yoga:

Movement, breath control, and meditation are all incorporated into these physical practices. They aid in stress reduction, flexibility improvement, and overall well-being.

7. Breathing: 4–7

Inhale for four counts, hold for seven counts, then exhale for eight counts. Dr. Andrew Weil popularized this breathing method, which is believed to produce calm and relieve stress.

8. Autogenic Conditioning:

Repeating a series of affirmations that encourage relaxation and bodily awareness is what autogenic training entails. To impact physical and mental feelings, phrases such as "my arms are heavy and warm" or "I am at peace" are employed.

Including Deep Breathing and Relaxation in Your Daily Routine

Consider the following practical advice to make the most of breathing and relaxation techniques:

Consistency: To reap the full benefits of these techniques, practice them on a regular basis, preferably everyday. Consistency is essential for obtaining long-term results.

Start Small: If you're new to these tactics, begin with shorter sessions and progressively increase their time as you gain confidence.

Combine Techniques: Experiment with several strategies to see which ones work best for you. You can also mix approaches to build your own relaxing routine.

Environment: Choose a distraction-free, peaceful area for your practice. This could be a separate room, a tranquil corner, or even a natural area.

Professional Coaching: Consider obtaining professional coaching from a competent instructor or therapist to assist you in developing your relaxation practice.

Breathing and relaxation techniques are not just quick fixes for temporary stress; they are long-term strategies for improving emotional well-being and resilience. By implementing these practices into your daily routine, you can achieve long-term inner peace, enhanced emotional regulation, and a stronger ability to face life's obstacles with grace and poise.

Meditation and mindfulness

Mindfulness and meditation emerge as important techniques for building mental clarity, emotional balance, and a deeper connection with yourself in a world characterized by continual activity, stress, and distraction. These practices have been used in numerous cultures for millennia and are now getting general acceptance for their excellent impact on mental and emotional well-being. Let's look at mindfulness and meditation, including definitions, advantages, and tips on how to incorporate them into your daily life.

Understanding Mindfulness: Being Present in the Moment

Mindfulness is a mental practice based on the ability to be present. It entails paying careful attention to the present moment and accepting it without judgment. Mindfulness allows you to become fully conscious of your thoughts, emotions, bodily sensations, and surroundings. It is about watching without attachment, accepting your experiences, and living in the present now.

Mindfulness Essentials:

Non-Judgment: Mindfulness teaches you to accept your ideas and feelings without judging them as correct or incorrect. This aids in the reduction of self-criticism and negative self-talk.

Observation: You become a bystander to your own experiences, allowing them to flow naturally. This impartiality allows you to gain a better grasp of your inner world.

Present Centered: Mindfulness emphasizes the value of being present in the moment rather than lingering on the past or worrying about the future.

Breath Awareness: Paying attention to your breath is a common way to begin practicing mindfulness. Concentrating on your breathing keeps you in the present moment and helps to quiet your mind.

Meditation: An Introduction

Meditation is a disciplined practice in which you focus your attention on a certain object, topic, or activity in order to gain mental clarity and emotional tranquility. Meditation includes a variety of techniques and traditions, but at its core, it is about training the mind to remain still and centered. It can be done while sitting, lying down, walking, or doing other ordinary tasks.

Common Meditation Methods:

Mindfulness meditation: As discussed earlier, mindfulness meditation emphasizes being totally present and aware of your thoughts, emotions, and sensations.

Transcendental Meditation: entails silently repeating a specific mantra in order to transcend mind and enter a deep state of relaxed awareness.

Loving-Kindness Meditation: Also known as Metta, cultivates feelings of love and compassion for yourself and others by repeating goodwill affirmations.

Guided Meditation: A guided meditation session is led by an instructor who provides verbal direction and visualization to help you relax and become more aware.

Body Scan Meditation: This technique involves focusing your attention on different regions of your body in a systematic manner, reducing tension and encouraging physical relaxation.

Meditation Has Many Advantages:

Stress Reduction: Meditation stimulates the relaxation response, lowering stress hormones and increasing calm.

Emotional Resilience: Meditation promotes emotional equilibrium, making it easier to handle unpleasant emotions and respond calmly to difficult situations.

Improved Concentration and Focus: Regular meditation improves attention and cognitive function, promoting productivity and clarity of thought.

Enhanced Sleep: Meditation can help you sleep better by calming your mind and lowering insomnia.

Pain Management: Mindfulness-based pain treatment, for example, can help lower pain perception and enhance pain tolerance.

Including Mindfulness and Meditation in Your Daily Life

Incorporating mindfulness and meditation into your everyday routine is simple and customizable to your own requirements. Here's where to begin:

Set a specified time aside each day for your mindfulness or meditation practice. Even just a few minutes can make a big difference. Create and locate a peaceful, comfortable area where you will not be bothered. Sit on a chair or cushion, lie down, or go for a contemplative walk in nature. Begin slowly, If you're new to these practices, start with short sessions and gradually increase the duration as you gain confidence. Select a technique, experiment with various meditation techniques to find one that works for you. There is no one-size-fits-all solution, so experiment to see what works best. Incorporate awareness into daily activities like eating, walking, or even dishwashing. Engage in these activities wholeheartedly and focus your attention on the current moment. Consistency is essential for enjoying the full benefits of mindfulness and meditation. Make it a daily ritual.

Mindfulness and meditation are not short cures, but rather lifelong practices that provide significant advantages to people who practice them. By incorporating these practices into your daily life, you can develop more self-awareness, emotional resilience, and inner serenity. These practices become anchors that keep you grounded, centered, and connected to your genuine self in the midst of life's demands and hardships.

The Effectiveness of Cognitive Behavioral Therapy (CBT)

Cognitive Behavioral Therapy (CBT) is a well-known and highly effective approach to mental health therapy. It is a structured, evidence-based psychotherapy that focuses on the interplay of thoughts, feelings, and behaviors. CBT is based on the concept that modifying negative thought patterns might result in better emotional well-being and healthier behaviors. Let's look at the ideas, practices, and benefits of Cognitive Behavioral Therapy.

Cognitive Behavioral Therapy Principles:

Cognition-Behavior Connection (CBT) is based on the idea that our ideas, emotions, and behaviors are all linked. Negative thought patterns can result in negative emotions and, as a result, undesirable behaviors. Try as much as possible to identify distorted thoughts. Cognitive behavioral therapy (CBT) assists individuals in Recognizing and challenging distorted or unreasonable thought processes, which are sometimes referred to as cognitive distortions. All-or-nothing thinking, catastrophizing, overgeneralization, and other distortions are examples of this. CBT also offers practical problem-solving skills that may be applied to real-life situations. It helps people to identify problems, make attainable goals, and create action plans.

CBT provides individuals with coping techniques to manage stress, anxiety, and other emotional issues. Relaxation techniques, assertiveness, and good communication are examples of these abilities.

CBT Strategies:

CBT uses a range of approaches to help people reframe their thoughts and improve their mental health:

Cognitive restructuring is detecting negative or distorted thought patterns and replacing them with more balanced and realistic views. Individuals can lessen anxiety and despair by confronting cognitive biases. CBT frequently incorporates practical experiments to verify the validity of negative beliefs. These experiments assist people in gathering evidence and shifting their perspectives.

Let's talk about "Exposure Therapy" which is a treatment method for phobias and anxiety disorders. It entails gradually exposing yourself to the dreaded object or scenario in order to diminish anxiety over time. Therapists frequently assign homework to reinforce skills and practices taught in therapy. This task encourages students to put new ways of thinking and acting into practice in real-life circumstances.

The Advantages of Cognitive Behavioural Therapy:

CBT is one of the most researched and validated techniques of psychotherapy, having a considerable body of data supporting its efficacy. CBT is a goal-oriented therapy, which makes it particularly useful for addressing specific concerns and delivering practical answers. CBT is frequently used as a short-term therapy, and many people see notable improvement after only a few sessions. CBT is adaptable for a variety of mental health issues, including anxiety disorders, depression, OCD, PTSD, eating disorders, and others. CBT provides clients with skills that they can use independently, allowing them to continue their progress outside of therapy. CBT can give long-term advantages by teaching people how to confront and reframe problematic thought patterns, resulting in more positive emotional experiences and better behaviors.

How to Start CBT:

If you're interested in CBT, here's how to get started:

Consult a skilled therapist, counselor, or psychologist who is knowledgeable about CBT. They will do an evaluation to evaluate whether CBT is appropriate for your individual needs. Work with your therapist to establish precise goals and expectations for your CBT treatment. Take an active role in the therapy process. Participate in the strategies and homework assignments prescribed by your therapist.

Maintain an open and honest contact with your therapist. Share your successes, difficulties, and any worries you have. Make sure you attend sessions on a regular basis and stick to the treatment plan. Consistency is essential for getting excellent results.

Cognitive Behavioural Therapy is a transforming method that has assisted countless people in regaining control of their mental health and leading more fulfilled lives. You can leverage CBT's ability to bring about positive transformation and emotional well-being by knowing its principles, strategies, and advantages and actively participating in the therapeutic process.

Self-Compassion and Acceptance

Self-compassion and self-acceptance serve as powerful reminders of the necessity of loving and nourishing one's inner self in a world that is often focused on external standards and perfection. These practices promote self-kindness and understanding, promoting emotional well-being, resilience, and a more positive relationship with one's own identity. , we will look at the meaning of self-compassion and self-acceptance, as well as the benefits they provide and how to implement them into your life.

Self-Compassion Explained:

Self-compassion entails treating yourself with the same compassion, care, and understanding that one would extend to a good friend. It is a self-love and self-care practice that aims to counterbalance the critical inner voice that frequently judges, condemns, or belittles yourself .

Self-compassion Is Comprised of Three Major Components:

Self-Kindness: Rather than harsh self-criticism, self-compassion entails being patient, understanding, and forgiving to yourself , particularly in times of adversity or failure. Self-compassion acknowledges that suffering and imperfection are part of the shared human experience. It serves as a reminder that we are not alone in our challenges.

Mindfulness: Self-compassion entails being aware of one's experiences without passing judgment on them. This thoughtful, non-judgmental approach provides for a more balanced understanding of one's thoughts and feelings.

Self-Compassion Has Many Advantages: Reduced Self-Criticism:

Self-compassion reduces the intensity of self-criticism and self-judgment, both of which can be harmful to one's mental health.

Improved Emotional Resilience: It increases emotional resilience by assisting individuals in more effectively coping with stress, adversity, and challenging emotions.

Enhanced Self-Esteem: Self-compassion fosters self-acceptance and self-love, which leads to higher self-esteem.

Greater Well-Being: According to research, people who practice self-compassion have higher levels of overall well-being, including less anxiety and sadness.

Understanding Self-Acknowledgement:

The practice of acknowledging and appreciating all aspects of yourself , including strengths, shortcomings, imperfections, and past mistakes, is known as self-acceptance. It entails developing a feeling of self-worth and self-love that is independent of external validation.

The Following Principles Underpin Self-acceptance:

Unconditional Self-Regard: Self-acceptance is not contingent on external achievements or the views of others. It is the ability to intrinsically esteem yourself .

Acceptance of Imperfection: Self-acceptance acknowledges that everyone is flawed and makes mistakes. It facilitates self-compassion and forgiveness.

Self-acceptance frees people to pursue personal growth and self-improvement without the burden of severe self-criticism.

Advantages of Self-Acceptance

Self-acceptance serves as a basis for emotional resilience, allowing individuals to endure hardship and disappointments more effectively. Anxiety can be reduced by accepting yourself as is, without the demand for perfection. Self-acceptance promotes self-confidence and self-worth, which promotes healthier, more real relationships. Self-acceptance is linked to higher life satisfaction, happiness, and general well-being.

Making Self-Compassion and Self-Acceptance a Part of Your Life

Take some time to think about your self-talk and mental patterns. Determine the areas in which self-compassion and self-acceptance are missing. When confronted with self-criticism or harsh judgements, replace negative self-talk with loving and understanding remarks. Treat yourself like you would a close friend. Establish a mindfulness practice that helps you to examine your thoughts and emotions without judgment. This practice can help you become more self-aware and compassionate. Also Recognize that you are a work in progress. Set attainable goals and accept the possibility of making mistakes along the way. Talk to a trustworthy friend, family member, or therapist about your journey towards self-compassion and self-acceptance. Their assistance and insights can be really beneficial. Make self-care activities that nourish your physical, emotional, and mental well-being a priority. This can include physical activity, meditation, hobbies, and relaxation.

Self-compassion and self-acceptance are continuing practices that can result in deep improvements in your connection with yourself and emotional well-being. You can go on a road to greater self-love, resilience, and personal growth by embracing and nourishing your inner self with kindness, understanding, and acceptance.

CHAPTER 4

Overcoming Specific Phobias

CONFRONTING YOUR FEARS

Fear is a strong emotion that may both protect and constrain us. While it frequently protects us from physical hazards, it can also prevent us from attaining our greatest potential and having a satisfying life. Facing your concerns is an important component of personal development since it can lead to greater self-confidence, resilience, and a sense of accomplishment. Let's look at the importance of facing your fears, as well as ways for doing so and the benefits it may bring to your life.

Overcoming Limitations:

The Importance of Facing Your Fears Fears can lead to self-imposed constraints that limit your chances and potential. Facing your anxieties can help to break down these obstacles and bring up new opportunities.

Confronting your anxieties aids in the development of emotional resilience. It teaches you how to manage and overcome difficult situations, making you better prepared to face hardship in the future.

Increasing Self-Confidence: Every time you face and overcome a fear, you earn a sense of accomplishment that contributes to increased self-confidence.

Personal Development: Facing phobias frequently requires moving outside of your comfort zone, which is where personal development and self-discovery occur.

Identify Your Fears: The first step in facing your fears is to identify what they are. Be precise about your fears, whether they are related to public speaking, heights, or social situations.

Analyze Your Fear: Examine your fear to determine its source and the underlying causes. This self-awareness can assist you in addressing the underlying causes of your fear.

Take Baby Steps: Rather than tackling your anxiety all at once, divide it into smaller, more manageable actions. Gradual exposure can help to make the process less intimidating.

Seek Help: Don't be reluctant to seek assistance or support from friends, family, or a therapist. Having someone to lean on can provide support and direction.

Use Relaxation Techniques: When confronted with fears, techniques such as deep breathing, meditation, or mindfulness can assist calm your mind and body.

Identify and question the negative attitudes and beliefs that are related to your worries. Replace them with more motivating and pleasant beliefs.

Visualize Success: Visualization can be a very effective approach. Visualize yourself successfully confronting and overcoming your fear, then play out this situation in your head.

The Advantages of Facing Your Fears

Increased Self-Esteem: Every time you face and overcome a fear, you boost your self-esteem and self-worth.

Facing phobias broadens your comfort zone, making you more adaptive and resilient in the face of obstacles.

Reduced Anxiety: Facing your anxieties might lead to less anxiety as you gain confidence in dealing with unpleasant situations.

New chances: By overcoming your anxieties, you open the door to previously unattainable chances and experiences.

Greater Independence: Facing your anxieties might help you become more self-sufficient and less dependent on others for reassurance and assistance.

Personal happiness: Facing your concerns can provide a tremendous sense of success and happiness.

Remember that confronting your anxieties is a process, and it's perfectly fine to take your time. The path may include setbacks and uncomfortable moments, but with determination and support, you can overcome your concerns and come out stronger on the other side. Facing your anxieties is ultimately an empowering act of self-discovery and personal progress that can lead to a more satisfying and fearless existence.

Exposition Therapy

Exposure therapy is a tried-and-true psychological treatment for anxiety disorders, phobias, and post-traumatic stress disorder (PTSD). It is based on the idea that confronting feared circumstances, objects, or ideas in a controlled and methodical manner helps reduce anxiety and increase emotional well-being. Let's look at the notion of exposure therapy, how it works, and how it might help people tackle their fears and worries.

Exposure therapy, also known as systematic desensitization, is a cognitive-behavioral strategy used to help people confront and overcome unreasonable fears and phobias. It entails exposing the individual to the feared stimuli (which could be a situation, item, or thinking) in a safe and controlled setting. The exposure is usually gradual and planned, with the purpose of gradually decreasing the individual's terror response.

How Does Exposure Therapy Work?

Assessment: Together, the therapist and the individual determine the precise fear or anxiety that needs to be treated. They talk about the feared stimulus and its causes.

The exposure hierarchy creates a hierarchy of feared circumstances or stimuli ranging from the least anxiety-provoking to the most anxiety-provoking. The exposure process is guided by this hierarchy.

Sessions of Exposure: The individual is gradually exposed to the things on the hierarchy, beginning with the least stressful and proceeding to increasingly difficult exposures. This can be done in the mind, in real life, or through virtual reality.

Response Prevention: During or after the exposure, the individual is urged to resist the impulse to engage in avoidance behaviors or routines (such as compulsions in OCD).

Exposure sessions are repeated over time to reinforce the learning that the feared stimuli are not as dangerous as initially thought. This repetition helps the individual desensitize to their worries.

Exposure Therapy Applications

Phobias: Exposure therapy is extremely successful for specific phobias such as fear of flying, heights, animals, or needles. People can gradually tackle their fears and minimize their uneasiness.

Exposure therapy can help people with social anxiety address circumstances that provoke their worries, such as public speaking, meeting new people, or attending social gatherings.

PTSD: Exposure therapy is frequently used to treat PTSD by assisting clients in confronting and processing painful memories and related triggers.

Exposure therapy is meant to expose individuals to events that trigger their obsessions, allowing them to resist the compulsions that follow.

Exposure therapy can be used to tackle specific worries and fears that contribute to generalized anxiety disorder.

Advantages of Exposure Therapy:

Anxiety Reduction: Exposure treatment is extremely effective at reducing anxiety and fear responses, allowing clients to restore emotional control.

Increased Confidence: When people tackle their fears and concerns, they typically gain self-confidence and a sense of empowerment.

Long-Term Relief: Exposure treatment can provide long-term relief from fears and anxieties, with many people reporting significant improvement after finishing the programme. Exposure therapy is dynamic and adaptive since it can be adjusted to the individual's personal anxieties and demands.

Fewer Avoidance Behaviors: People frequently report fewer avoidance behaviors, which leads to increased participation in everyday activities and a higher quality of life.

Exposure therapy is a methodical and evidence-based strategy that can assist people in confronting their fears and worries, ultimately leading to a more fulfilled and empowered existence. If you are experiencing unjustified concerns or anxiety, talk to a mental health practitioner about the potential advantages of exposure treatment tailored to your specific requirements.

Gradual Desensitization

Gradual desensitization is an effective therapy strategy for helping people address and overcome irrational fears, phobias, and anxiety in a systematic and controlled manner. It is based on exposure treatment and cognitive-behavioral therapy concepts, and it entails a step-by-step process of desensitizing a person to a feared stimuli or circumstance. Let's look at the notion of gradual desensitization, how it works, and how it might be used to treat anxiety and phobias.

Gradual desensitization, also known as systematic desensitization, is a therapy technique for diminishing anxiety and terror linked with specific items, events, or ideas. It entails gradually exposing the individual to the dreaded stimuli, beginning with less anxiety-provoking events and progressing to more difficult ones. The primary goal is to assist the individual in developing confidence and reducing their emotional response to fear-inducing events.

Gradual Desensitization in Action:

Fear Identification: Identifying the specific fear or phobia that needs to be treated is the first stage in the procedure. Flying, spiders, heights, or public speaking are all possibilities.

The Fear Hierarchy: A hierarchy of dreaded scenarios or stimuli is formed, with things ranked from least to most anxiety-inducing. This hierarchy guides the gradual exposure procedure.

Relaxation Techniques: Prior to the start of the exposure, the participant is given relaxation techniques such as deep breathing, gradual muscular relaxation, and awareness. These approaches assist the individual in managing their anxiousness throughout the process.

Step-by-Step Exposure: The subject is gradually exposed to the fear-inducing stimuli, beginning with the least anxiety-provoking item in the hierarchy. Exposure can occur through imagination, in real-life settings, or even through the use of virtual reality.

Controlled and Safe atmosphere: Exposure must take place in a controlled and safe atmosphere, and the individual must be encouraged to face their fear voluntarily.

Response Prevention: During or after the exposure, the individual is advised not to engage in avoidance behaviors or rituals (compulsions in cases of OCD). This is critical for lowering the anxiety response.

Progressive Advancement: As the individual successfully faces the less stressful elements on the hierarchy, they advance to increasingly difficult exposures. The idea is to gradually desensitize them to their fear.

Gradual Desensitisation Applications:

Specific Phobias: For specific phobias such as fear of flying, animals, public speaking, or restricted areas, gradual desensitization is quite helpful.

It can assist those who suffer from social anxiety in confronting circumstances that trigger their social phobias, such as speaking in public, attending social events, or initiating conversations.

Post-Traumatic Stress Disorder (PTSD): Gradual desensitization is frequently used to treat trauma-related triggers in those suffering from PTSD.

Individuals suffering from generalized anxiety might use it to address specific worries and anxieties that contribute to their condition.

Advantages of Gradual Desensitization:

Anxiety Reduction: Gradual desensitization is extremely effective at reducing anxiety and fear responses, allowing people to regain emotional control.

Empowerment: When people face their anxieties in a systematic way and succeed, they typically develop a sense of empowerment and self-confidence.

Long-Term Relief: Gradual desensitization can provide long-term relief from phobias and anxiety, with many people reporting significant improvement after finishing the procedure.

It is a flexible and adaptive strategy since it can be adjusted to an individual's specific worries and demands.

Reduced Avoidance Behaviors: Gradual desensitization frequently results in decreased avoidance behaviors, promoting better engagement in daily activities and a higher quality of life.

Gradual desensitization is a well-established and efficient therapy strategy that allows people to face their anxieties and phobias in a systematic manner. If you suffer from unwarranted fears or anxiety, talk to a mental health expert about the benefits of gradual desensitization suited to your unique requirements.

True Stories

Anxiety and phobias are strong obstacles that can have a substantial impact on a person's life. Many people, however, have tackled harsh challenges head on, displaying great resilience and determination. Their success stories serve as beacons of hope and inspiration, demonstrating that anxiety and phobias may be conquered and lead fulfilling lives. Let's look at a few incredible success stories of people who overcame their anxieties and phobias.

1. Sarah - Overcoming Social Anxiety: For most of her life, Sarah struggled with social anxiety, making it difficult for her to engage in social interactions, attend gatherings, or even speak in public. Sarah sought treatment and gradually exposed herself to social situations in order to overcome her nervousness. She gradually regained her confidence through cognitive-behavioral therapy and the support of loved ones. Sarah is now a mental health champion who frequently talks at public events, sharing her story and assisting others in overcoming social anxiety.

2. John - Overcoming phobia of Flying:

John suffered from a terrible phobia of flying, which kept him from achieving his dream of traveling the world. He decided to get treatment and began exposure therapy to progressively tackle his phobia. He began with modest flights and gradually increased his distance with the help of a therapist. Now, John travels with confidence and has visited places he never imagined imaginable.

3. Lisa - Overcoming Agoraphobia: Lisa suffered from agoraphobia, which made it difficult for her to leave the house. For years, her worry had kept her alone. She went on a gradual desensitization journey with the help of a therapist. Lisa began by taking little visits around her neighborhood and gradually broadened her horizons. She now appreciates the freedom to go wherever she wants and cherishes every time spent outside her home.

4. Mark - Overcoming Arachnophobia:

Mark's terrible arachnophobia paralyzed him at the sight of a spider. He chose exposure treatment to face his phobia, gradually exposing himself to photos, movies, and, eventually, live spiders. Mark learnt to handle his fear through regular and controlled exposures. He can now coexist peacefully with these eight-legged critters.

5. Emma - Thriving Despite exam Anxiety:

Emma suffered from crippling exam anxiety, which hampered her academic achievement. She sought treatment and acquired relaxation techniques to assist her control her anxiety throughout exams. Emma stayed calm and focused by practicing mindfulness and deep breathing. Her increased abilities enabled her to flourish academically and secure her ideal career.

6. David - Overcoming Public Speaking phobia:

David longed to be a motivational speaker despite his phobia of public speaking. He began a process of gradual desensitization and exposure therapy. He began by speaking in front of a mirror, then to a close friend, and eventually expanded his audience. David overcame his nervousness through perseverance and practice, and he is now a sought-after public speaker.

These triumphs highlight the transforming power of resilience, persistence, and evidence-based therapy in overcoming anxiety and phobias. They show how, with the correct help and progressive exposure, people can break free from the confines of their anxieties and recover their lives. These stories provide hope and inspiration to anyone suffering from anxiety or phobias, demonstrating that a brighter, worry-free future is possible.

CHAPTER 5

Social Anxiety

UNDERSTANDING SOCIAL ANXIETY

Social anxiety, a common but frequently misunderstood emotion, can cast a cloud over one's social encounters, impeding one's capacity to freely participate and connect with others. In Chapter 5, we look into the complicated landscape of social anxiety, giving light on its origins, symptoms, and successful coping mechanisms.

What Causes Social Anxiety?

At its foundation, social anxiety is an extreme fear of being judged, embarrassed, or negatively evaluated in social circumstances. While it manifests differently in each individual, its origins are frequently traced back to a combination of genetic, environmental, and psychological variables. Individuals suffering with social anxiety may be overly sensitive to perceived criticism, resulting in a continuous worry of saying or doing something socially unacceptable.

Symptoms of Social Anxiety

The indications of social anxiety can be varied and significant. Physical sensations such as blushing, trembling, sweating, and a racing heart are frequently related with the emotional turmoil involved with social encounters. Individuals suffering with social anxiety may go to tremendous measures to avoid situations that cause them discomfort, resulting in social isolation and missed opportunities for personal and professional development.

The Mental Aspect

Cognitive distortions are important in social anxiety. Anxiety is exacerbated by negative thought patterns such as catastrophic thinking or an overestimation of the likelihood of social blunders. These mistaken perceptions feed a self-reinforcing loop in which the fear of being judged negatively becomes a self-fulfilling prophecy.

The Effect on Everyday Life

Social anxiety can impair not just social interactions, but also academic and professional goals. Simple acts such as making a phone call, attending social gatherings, or participating in meetings can become daunting hurdles for people who suffer from social anxiety. The pervasiveness of this illness emphasizes the significance of thorough treatment.

Understanding the Spectrum

It's critical to understand that social anxiety is a spectrum disorder, with symptoms ranging from minor discomfort to severe impairment. While some people may suffer periodic uneasiness in social circumstances, others may avoid social contacts entirely. Understanding this spectrum is critical for personalizing interventions to the specific requirements of individuals at various positions on the social anxiety spectrum.

In the Age of Technology, Social Anxiety

Social anxiety has found new ways to exhibit itself in the digital era. For some, the pressure to maintain a managed online identity, combined with the dread of being judged in the virtual arena, can increase social anxiety. The separation of one's digital and offline selves can lead to emotional struggle and increased isolation from true social interactions.

Effective Social Anxiety Management Techniques

While social anxiety can be difficult to manage, there are effective ways for reducing its effects. Cognitive-behavioral therapy (CBT), exposure therapy, and mindfulness-based approaches have demonstrated potential in assisting people to reframe negative thought patterns, gradually encounter frightening circumstances, and cultivate present-moment awareness.

Developing Social Skills

Developing and polishing social skills is an important element of dealing with social anxiety. Active listening, maintaining eye contact, and understanding how to navigate small chat are all examples of this.

Individuals can boost their confidence in social situations and minimize their dread of interpersonal interactions by systematically developing these abilities.

The Influence of Self-Compassion

Accepting self-compassion is a transformative step in overcoming social anxiety. Recognizing that everyone feels embarrassed or self-conscious in social circumstances might help to relieve the pressure to be flawless. Individuals might gradually rethink their relationship with social encounters by treating themselves with care and empathy.

Seeking Professional Assistance

Seeking professional help is a critical step for many people in dealing with social anxiety. Therapists and mental health specialists can offer targeted solutions, a secure environment for investigation, and assistance in establishing coping skills. In some circumstances, medication may be prescribed to address underlying symptoms and promote therapeutic progress.

Creating a Positive Environment

Individuals dealing with social anxiety must create a supportive social environment. Friends, family, and coworkers may make a tremendous difference by encouraging inclusivity, offering support, and recognizing the difficulties that persons with social anxiety encounter. Open communication and a nonjudgmental attitude can make a significant difference.

Understanding social anxiety entails delving into its foundations, symptoms, and successful management measures. Individuals can engage on a journey of self-discovery and empowerment by understanding the spectrum of social anxiety, admitting its influence on daily life, and adopting helpful interventions. We create the road for more empathy, lower stigma, and a more inclusive social landscape in which everyone can prosper honestly.

Building Social Skills

One of the main threads in the rich tapestry of managing social anxiety is the development and refinement of social skills. These abilities serve as the foundation for people suffering from social anxiety to gain confidence, navigate social encounters, and develop meaningful connections. In Chapter 5, we dig into the transforming path of developing social skills, recognizing it as a necessary step in overcoming the obstacles of social anxiety.

Recognizing Social Skills

Social skills are a collection of behaviors and talents that allow for productive and harmonious relationships with others. These abilities include the art of communication, active listening, interpreting nonverbal clues, and negotiating the unspoken laws of social engagement. Individuals suffering from social anxiety will find that strengthening these abilities is a valuable tool for breaking down boundaries and creating genuine connections.

Social Anxiety's Influence on Social Skills

Social anxiety is frequently a strong impediment to the normal development of social skills. The fear of being judged, negatively evaluated, or making a social faux pas might prevent people from acting truthfully in social circumstances. This avoidance might result in a stagnation of social skills, stifling personal and professional development.

The Lack of Social Skills

Individuals suffering from social anxiety may have a social skills deficiency, which means that their ability to negotiate diverse social cues and standards is undeveloped. This impairment can be exhibited by difficulties initiating discussions, maintaining eye contact, interpreting facial expressions, and engaging in small chat. Addressing this impairment is a critical component of properly managing social anxiety.

Desensitization in a systematic manner

The process of developing social skills is known as systematic desensitization. This treatment strategy enables patients to address and gradually overcome their phobias by gradually exposing themselves to social circumstances. Starting with less daunting settings and gradually progressing to more difficult interactions allows for the gradual development of social skills.

Listening Actively

Active listening is a key social skill that requires the ability to completely concentrate, hear, and respond to what someone is saying. Active listening can be a useful practice for people who suffer from social anxiety. They can improve their capacity to connect with others and contribute effectively to conversations by focusing on the speaker rather than internal concerns.

Communication without using words

Another important part of developing social skills is understanding and efficiently using nonverbal communication. Maintaining acceptable body language, deciphering facial expressions, and being aware of one's own nonverbal clues are all part of this. Nonverbal communication practice can help people show confidence and openness in social situations.

Starting and Maintaining Conversations

For people who suffer from social anxiety, it can be difficult to establish and continue discussions. Developing conversation starters, asking open-ended questions, and actively participating in group conversations are all ways to improve your social skills in this area. Gradual exposure to social situations allows for practice of these abilities in a safe atmosphere.

Making Small Talk

While small talk may appear insignificant, it serves as a springboard to deeper interactions. Individuals suffering from social anxiety can benefit from learning the art of small talk, which entails identifying common ground, displaying genuine interest, and effortlessly navigating discussions. Activities that build skills, such as practicing with a trusted buddy, can help you grow confidence in this area.

Receiving and Giving Positive Feedback

The development of social skills is an ongoing process that requires a willingness to listen and provide constructive feedback. Constructive criticism is an opportunity for growth, not a reflection of personal failure. Having an open mind when receiving feedback promotes constant progress in social relations.

Simulation and role-playing

Role-playing and social simulations are helpful techniques for developing social skills in a controlled context. Participating in these tasks with a therapist, support group, or trusted friend provides a secure environment for practice and feedback without the pressure of real-life repercussions.

Seeking Professional Help

Seeking professional help when dealing with social anxiety is an important step in the process of developing social skills. Anxiety disorder therapists can provide specific solutions, assistance, and a systematic framework for social skill improvement. Professional assistance provides a secure and empathetic atmosphere in which to confront obstacles and appreciate triumphs.

Building social skills is a life-changing process that enables those who suffer from social anxiety to negotiate the intricacies of social relationships with confidence and sincerity. Individuals can unleash the potential for meaningful connections and a more rewarding social life by actively engaging in skill-building activities, seeking exposure to social settings, and accepting continual growth. This path is about creating a foundation for a future filled with genuine connections, personal growth, and a sense of social fulfillment, not just overcoming social anxiety.

Social Situational Strategies

The chapter on social anxiety methods emerges as a guide through the maze of dread and self-doubt in the complicated dance of controlling social anxiety. Social encounters, which are sometimes frightening for people who have social anxiety, become chances for growth, connection, and the progressive breakdown of the walls that prevent genuine engagement. Let's look at a wide range of tactics designed to empower people in social situations, allowing them to confidently traverse the intricacies.

Planning and Visualization

In the fight against social anxiety, preparation is a strong ally. Take some time before entering a social environment to positively visualize the event. Imagine yourself easily navigating conversations, expressing yourself, and enjoying the company of people. This mental rehearsal might assist to reframe negative expectations and inspire confidence.

Set realistic goals for yourself.

Setting reasonable expectations is essential for dealing with social anxiety. Accept that not every interaction must be flawless, and that it is normal to feel uncomfortable at times. Accept the notion that social situations are opportunities for development rather than examinations with a pass/fail conclusion.

Gradual Exposition

Gradual exposure is a key method for dealing with social anxiety. Begin with smaller, less daunting social encounters and work your way up to more difficult scenarios. This step-by-step strategy allows for acclimatization, which aids in the development of confidence and the reduction of worry over time.

Make use of Relaxation Techniques

In order to treat physical symptoms of anxiety, incorporate relaxation practices. Deep breathing techniques, progressive muscular relaxation, and mindfulness can all help to quiet the nervous system and help you navigate social situations with a clear and focused mind.

Create Exit Strategies

It is natural to feel overwhelmed in a social setting, and having exit methods in place provides a safety net. Identify a quiet area where you can withdraw if necessary, or communicate with a trusted friend that you may require some alone time. Knowing you have an exit strategy can help you relax.

Concentrate on Others

A great tactic is to divert one's attention away from oneself. Instead than obsessing on internal concerns, concentrate on others in a social context.

Pose open-ended inquiries, attentively listen to their answers, and demonstrate real interest. Shifting the emphasis outside can help to alleviate self-consciousness.

Accept Imperfection

Perfection is an impossible goal. Accept the beauty of imperfection, acknowledging that everyone has awkward social situations. Allow for mistakes and embrace them as learning and growth opportunities rather than causes of shame.

Make Small Goals

Divide societal challenges into doable objectives. Setting tiny, attainable goals, whether it's starting a conversation, creating eye contact, or participating in a group discussion, allows for incremental development. Celebrate every accomplishment, no matter how tiny, to foster a sense of accomplishment.

Participate in Social Skills Training

Social skills training, whether delivered in a therapy context or through structured courses, gives tailored direction for improving interpersonal skills. These classes provide practical activities, role-playing, and constructive feedback to gradually strengthen and refine social skills.

Negative Thoughts Must Be Challenged

Negative thoughts might contribute to social anxiety. Challenge and reframe these thoughts by determining whether they are founded on evidence or unreasonable worries. Replace negative self-talk with more balanced, realistic ideas to positively transform your thinking.

Create a Support System

Create a supportive network of friends, family, or peers that understand and sympathize with your situation. In social situations, having a trusted support system provides encouragement, validation, and a sense of connection.

Make Use of Humor

In social contexts, humor may be a strong tool. A well-timed joke, self-deprecating humor, or a shared chuckle can help to relieve tension and create a more relaxed environment.

Active listening should be practiced.

Active listening is a valuable social skill that encourages participation and connection. Keep your attention on the speaker, nod in agreement, and react wisely. Active listening improves social connections while also diverting attention away from internal fears.

Positive Experiences Teach Us

Consider your favorable social encounters. Identify examples where social interactions went successfully and investigate what factors contributed to the positive outcomes. Success tales might provide useful insights and boost confidence for future meetings.

Commemorate Progress

It is critical to recognize and celebrate progress. Every step in overcoming social anxiety is a victory. Reflect on problems overcome, no matter how minor, and acknowledge progress made in social contexts.

Participate in Group Activities

Group activities provide an organized atmosphere for social interaction. Joining a club, class, or social group centered on shared interests provides common ground and facilitates connections with others.

Prioritize quality over quantity.

In social situations, quality encounters frequently outnumber quantity. Rather than striving to engage a vast crowd, concentrate on making genuine connections with a few people. Quality relationships have a substantial impact on overall social satisfaction.

Create a Personal Mantra

Make a customized mantra or affirmation to help you feel more confident in social situations. Positive remarks that enhance self-worth and capability should be repeated. Internalizing these affirmations can be a source of strength during difficult times.

Seek Professional Help

When social anxiety causes major difficulties, obtaining professional help is a proactive step. Anxiety disorder therapists can provide specific methods, coping skills, and support to help you handle social situations with confidence.

Consider and Learn

Take some-time after social interactions to reflect on the event. Determine what went well, what may be improved, and any negative ideas that surfaced. Use these reflections as opportunities for ongoing learning and development.

The solutions mentioned for social situations assist persons dealing with social anxiety with a comprehensive toolkit. Individuals can shift social contacts from sources of dread to opportunities for connection, personal development, and a meaningful social life by gradually implementing these tactics. Remember that the path to confident social interaction is unique to each person, and progress demonstrates strength and perseverance in the face of social anxiety.

Real-Life Testimonials:

Overcoming Social Anxiety Using Applied Strategies

Real-life testimonials serve as tremendous beacons of hope and inspiration in the transforming journey of overcoming social anxiety. Individuals who have overcome social anxiety by implementing the tactics provided in this section provide insights into the enormous influence these strategies can have on one's life. Let us delve into their triumphant, resilient, and successful experiences, demonstrating how social setting tactics have become catalysts for good transformation.

Sarah's Confidence Journey

Sarah, a vivacious young professional, recalls vividly her battles with social anxiety, which hampered her job possibilities. Her aversion to networking events, team meetings, and speeches hampered her career development. Dedicated to breaking free from the confines of social anxiety.

Sarah's Applied Techniques

- Gradual Exposure: Sarah began by attending small team meetings and advanced to larger presentations over time.
- Active Listening: During group talks, she focused on active listening to divert her attention away from self-conscious thoughts.

- Establish Realistic Expectations: Sarah learnt to establish realistic expectations for social interactions, leaving room for error.

The End Result

Sarah's confidence grew with time. She negotiated team interactions with ease, enthusiastically participating in conversations. Her acquired abilities not only advanced her job but also improved her entire well-being. Sarah's accomplishment demonstrates the transforming impact of progressive exposure and attentive listening in professional contexts.

Mark Social Renaissance

Mark, a college student, was plagued by social anxiety, which made it difficult for him to connect with his peers. Mark, who was afraid of social occasions, resolved to implement the tactics to regain his social life.

Applied Strategies by Mark

- Gradual Exposure: Mark began by visiting small social gatherings with close friends before progressing to larger events.

- Use Relaxation Techniques: To treat physical symptoms of anxiety, he added deep breathing exercises.

- Accept Imperfection: Mark questioned the concept of perfection and allowed himself to make mistakes without condemnation.

The End Result

Mark's social rebirth was astounding. He participated in a variety of social events, building relationships with peers and broadening his social circle. The use of relaxation techniques gave a steadying influence during encounters, and embracing imperfection allowed him to enjoy social situations without the weight of unreasonable expectations.

Emily's Social Life Has Been Reimagined

Emily, a young adult, struggled with social anxiety, which made ordinary interactions difficult. Her dread of being judged and rejected hampered her personal relationships. Emily set out on a quest to rebuild her social life.

Emily's Applied Strategies

- Develop exit plans: Emily created escape plans to help her cope with overwhelming social settings.
- Set Small Goals: She established tiny, attainable goals for starting conversations and maintaining eye contact.
- Prioritize Quality Over Quantity: Emily prioritized deep connections with a few close friends over a vast social circle.

The End Result

Emily's social life made a significant change. Her ability to gracefully exit difficult circumstances emboldened her, and setting minor goals gave concrete progress markers. Emily created meaningful connections by stressing quality over quantity, which added to her overall sense of satisfaction and fulfillment.

James' Professional Victory

Due to social anxiety, James, a seasoned professional in a corporate context, struggled with networking and team interactions. Recognizing the impact on his profession, James dedicated himself to applying social setting tactics.

Applied Strategies by James

- Before corporate events and speeches, James did extensive preparation and visualization.
- He attended social skills training programs to improve his interpersonal skills.
- To reinforce effective techniques, James frequently reflected on favorable social interactions.

The End Result

James' professional success was obvious. His ability to confidently handle corporate settings resulted in increasing prominence and recognition. James not only conquered professional hurdles but also became a role model for his coworkers by embracing social skills training and learning from positive experiences.

Mia's Self-Discovery Journey

Mia, a young woman dealing with social anxiety in numerous facets of her life, set out on a path of self-discovery and progress. Mia improved her relationship with social encounters by implementing these tried-and-true techniques.

Mia's Practical Strategies

- To enhance her confidence and encourage positive self-talk, Mia devised a personal mantra.
- She actively engaged with people in social settings, shifting her focus away from internal concerns.
- Mia recognized and appreciated her growth by celebrating every minor milestone.

The End Result

Mia's self-discovery quest resulted in renewed self-confidence and sincerity. She established meaningful connections that resonated with her ideals by crafting a personal motto and focused on others. Mia's tale exemplifies the transforming power of recognizing one's success and embracing one's individual journey.

These real-life examples demonstrate the transforming effect of social setting tactics in the context of social anxiety management. Each tale demonstrates the dedication, perseverance, and growth of individuals who used these tactics to overcome the hurdles posed by social anxiety. Their victories attest to the efficacy of gradual exposure, active listening, and other tactics in creating confidence, connection, and a revitalized sense of self. As these people thrive, their experiences encourage others on similar paths to go on a path of self-discovery, perseverance, and triumph over social anxiety.

CHAPTER 6

Dealing with Panic Attack

WHAT ARE PANIC ATTACKS?

Panic attacks are acute, frightening events that can be quite stressful for people who suffer from them. Understanding what it's like inside a panic attack is critical for providing support and understanding to those going through this difficult struggle. Let's look at a panic attack from the inside to provide light on the overwhelming nature of this phenomenon.

1. Extreme Fear and Anxiety:

A panic episode is characterized by a rapid and severe surge of fear and worry. It's as if the world around you has become a menace, and you have no way of escaping it. Fear is frequently unreasonable and far more strong than the circumstance merits.

2. Physical Signs and Symptoms:

A panic episode can cause a variety of distressing physical symptoms, including:

Rapid Heartbeat: Your heart is racing and may feel like it's hammering out of your chest.

Breathlessness: You struggle to catch your breath, frequently hyperventilating.

Sweating: Excessive sweating can occur, which can be uncomfortable.

Uncontrollable trembling or shaking: Your body may shake uncontrollably.

Chest discomfort or Discomfort: Some people have chest discomfort, which might be misinterpreted as a heart attack.

Dizziness and lightheadedness: You may feel as if you are going to pass out.

Nausea or stomach discomfort: Nausea or stomach discomfort is prevalent.

Tingling or Numbness: Your extremities may tingle or feel numb.

Choking sensation: Some people believe they are being strangled or suffocated.

3. Psychological Symptoms: Panic episodes can cause psychological symptoms such as:

Fear of Loss of Control: You may believe that you are losing control of your body or thoughts.

Unreality: The world may appear surreal or dreamy.

Detachment from Reality: You may feel separated from your surroundings, as if you're seeing in the mirror.

Fear of Losing Your Mind: Panic attacks can cause a strong fear of losing your mind.

4. Duration and Intensity: Panic episodes typically last a few minutes but can linger up to half an hour. A panic attack's severity might vary, with some people having more severe symptoms than others. Individuals may feel fatigued and emotionally exhausted after a panic episode.

5. Fear of Future Attacks: One of the most difficult components of having a panic attack is the fear of having another one. This dread can be a persistent source of anxiety, leading to avoidance behaviors in which people avoid situations or places where they've had a panic attack in the past.

6. Impact on Daily Life: Panic attacks can severely interrupt a person's life, making it difficult to engage in daily activities, employment, social contacts, and even routine tasks such as grocery shopping or driving.

7. Seeking Help: Many people who suffer from panic attacks finally seek help from mental health specialists. Therapy, medication, and coping methods can all aid in the management and prevention of future attacks.

Understanding a panic attack is critical for loved ones and support networks. Empathy, reassurance, and understanding can be quite beneficial in assisting folks in coping with the challenges of panic attacks. It is also critical for persons who suffer from panic attacks to get expert assistance and treatment in order to manage and overcome this terrible condition.

Seeking Professional Assistance

Therapy's Transformative Role in Managing Anxiety and Phobias

Therapy can help people suffering from anxiety and phobias recover control of their life and find relief from their terrible symptoms. Mental health experts provide crucial support, guidance, and skills to those dealing with these issues, whether through cognitive-behavioral therapy (CBT), exposure therapy, or other therapeutic approaches. Let's look at how therapy can help you manage your anxiety and phobias.

1. Recognizing and Understanding Triggers: Therapists work with clients to identify the precise triggers that cause anxiety and phobia symptoms. The first step in building effective coping methods is to identify these triggers.

2. Cognitive-Behavioral Therapy (CBT): CBT is one of the most extensively utilized and successful anxiety and phobia treatments. It focuses on Recognizing and addressing unreasonable thought processes that cause worry. Individuals learn to reframe their thoughts, replace irrational beliefs with rational ones, and cultivate healthy ways of thinking.

3. Exposure Therapy: Exposure therapy is especially useful for phobias. It entails gradually and carefully exposing yourself to the feared stimuli or scenario. Individuals grow desensitized to their worries over time, lessening the severity of their phobia.

4. Coping skills: Therapists offer a variety of coping skills to help people control their anxiety and phobia symptoms. Deep breathing exercises, mindfulness practices, and progressive muscular relaxation are examples of such strategies.

5. Self-Assessment: Therapists frequently lead clients through self-assessment exercises to help them get insight into their anxieties and phobias. This self-awareness is essential for understanding triggers and establishing tailored coping techniques.

6. Developing Resilience: Therapy can help people develop resilience and emotional strength. It gives them the tools they need to manage difficult circumstances and deal with stress more successfully.

7. Setting Realistic Goals: Therapists help people set realistic and achievable goals for dealing with anxiety and phobias. These objectives serve as a road map for success and improvement.

8. Empathy and Support: The therapy interaction itself provides support and empathy. Individuals suffering from anxiety and phobias frequently feel lonely, but therapy provides a secure place for them to communicate their fears and concerns.

9. Medication Management: Therapy may be supplemented in some situations by medication recommended by a healthcare practitioner. Therapists can collaborate with medical specialists to ensure that medicine is utilized correctly.

10. Relapse Prevention: Therapists assist patients with developing relapse prevention plans. These plans detail tactics for Recognizing, treating, and preventing future anxiety and phobia attacks.

11. Holistic Approaches: Holistic approaches to treatment, such as yoga, mindfulness, and relaxation techniques, may be used by therapists. These can be used in addition to established therapy procedures.

12. Tailored Treatment: One of therapy's greatest benefits is its capacity to be extremely personalized. Therapists customize treatment regimens to each person's specific needs, triggers, and symptoms.

In conclusion, therapy is essential in the treatment of anxiety and phobias. It provides individuals with the knowledge and resources they need to confront their concerns, question irrational thinking, and create healthier coping mechanisms. Therapy's transforming influence extends beyond symptom treatment to allowing patients to reclaim control of their lives and find relief from the uncomfortable symptoms of anxiety and phobias.

Medication and Alternative Treatment Options for Anxiety and Phobias

Anxiety and phobias are frequently treated with a combination of medicine and alternative therapies. While medication can provide symptom relief, alternative treatments can help individuals improve coping skills and address underlying concerns. Let's look at the roles of medicine and other treatment choices in the treatment of anxiety and phobias.

1. Medicine:

a. Anti-Anxiety Drugs:

Benzodiazepines (e.g., Xanax, Ativan) can provide immediate relief from acute anxiety symptoms. They function by relaxing the central nervous system.

Considerations: Because these drugs can become habit-forming, they are normally only prescribed for short-term use to treat severe anxiety attacks.

b. Antidepressant medications:

Anxiety disorders are routinely treated with selective serotonin reuptake inhibitors (SSRIs) and serotonin-norepinephrine reuptake inhibitors (SNRIs). They reduce anxiety by helping to control serotonin and norepinephrine levels in the brain.

Considerations: It may take several weeks for antidepressants to take effect, and side effects can vary. To monitor their use, it is critical to collaborate closely with a healthcare expert.

c. Beta-Blocking Agents:

Role: Beta-blockers (for example, propranolol) are sometimes recommended to treat physical symptoms of anxiety, such as racing heart and shaking. They are frequently used in specific settings, such as public speaking.

Considerations: Because these drugs primarily treat physical symptoms, they are not appropriate for all types of anxiety or phobias.

2. Other Therapeutic Options:

a. CBT (Cognitive-Behavioral Therapy):

CBT is an evidence-based therapy that assists patients in identifying and challenging illogical thought processes that contribute to anxiety. It is quite effective in treating a variety of anxiety and phobia problems.

b. Exposition Therapy:

Exposure treatment is very beneficial for specific phobias. It entails gradually and controlled exposure to the dreaded stimulus, gradually diminishing the severity of the phobia.

c.   Techniques   for   Mindfulness   and Relaxation:

Role: Mindfulness exercises and relaxation techniques, such as deep breathing and progressive muscle relaxation, aid in the management of anxiety and phobia symptoms by encouraging relaxation and stress reduction.

d. Support Organizations:

Support groups serve as a source of community and understanding. Sharing experiences with people who are going through similar difficulties can be both validating and reassuring.

e. Holistic Methodologies:

Yoga, acupuncture, aromatherapy, and herbal supplements can all be used to support established therapeutic procedures. While not a major remedy, they may aid in the management of anxiety symptoms.

f. Lifestyle Modifications:

A healthy lifestyle that includes regular exercise, balanced eating, appropriate sleep, and stress management is essential for general mental well-being and anxiety management.

h. Self-Help Literature and Resources:

Self-help books, apps, and online resources can give individuals skills and guidance to better understand and manage their anxiety and phobias.

3. Combining Medication with Alternative Treatments:

To effectively manage anxiety and phobias, it is usual for people to employ a combination of medication and other treatments. Medication can alleviate acute symptoms, allowing people to participate in therapy and learn coping methods. Individuals may gradually reduce or quit medication under the supervision of a healthcare practitioner as they develop resilience and coping abilities.

The treatment chosen is determined on the precise diagnosis, the individual's unique demands, and their choices. Working together with a mental health professional to develop the optimal treatment plan and evaluate progress is critical for achieving the best potential outcomes for controlling anxiety and phobias.

CHAPTER 7

Self-Care and Lifestyle

FINDING THE RIGHT THERAPIST

Finding the proper therapist is an important step towards improving mental health and emotional well-being. Whether you seek therapy for anxiety, phobias, or any other issue, the therapeutic relationship is essential to successful treatment. In this articleLet's go over the steps and factors to consider when looking for a therapist.

1. Identify Your Needs:

Before you start looking, you should figure out what you want out of treatment. Take into account your individual issues, goals, and preferences. Are you looking for help with anxiety or a specific phobia? Do you have a specific therapy strategy in mind? Understanding your requirements will help you narrow down your search.

2. Obtain Referrals:

Primary care physicians frequently make referrals to mental health providers. They can make recommendations depending on your individual needs. Request therapist referrals from others in your network. Personal recommendations can be extremely beneficial.

3. Investigate and Research:

Online Therapist Directories and Databases: Use online therapist directories and databases to find therapists in your area. Websites such as Psychology Today and GoodTherapy might be useful resources. Many professional organizations, such as the American Psychological Association (APA) or the National Association of Social Workers (NASW), provide therapist directories.

4. Verify Credentials:

Check if the therapist is licensed and has the necessary qualifications. Look for titles like Licenced Clinical Social Worker (LCSW), Licenced Professional Counsellor (LPC), Psychologist (Ph.D. or Psy.D.), and Psychiatrist (M.D.). Check their credentials with your state's licensing board.

5. Think about Specialization:

If you're looking for therapy for a specific issue, such as anxiety or phobias, look for therapists who have experience and competence in treating those issues. Therapy can be made more successful by specializing.

6. Investigate Therapeutic Approaches:

Various therapy approaches (for example, CBT, psychoanalysis, and mindfulness) are used by different therapists. Learn about various ways so you may select one that fits your interests and goals.

7. Speak with Potential Therapists:

Request a quick phone or in-person consultation with possible therapists. This initial talk might assist you in determining their approach, demeanor, and how well you might work together.

8. Think about logistics:

Consider where the therapist's office is located. Is it easy for you to get to? Do you want in-person or online therapy?

Availability: Confirm that the therapist's schedule matches yours and that they can accommodate your preferred appointment hours.

9. Follow Your Instincts:

Finally, the appropriate therapist is someone with whom you feel at ease and secure. During the first meeting, trust your instincts. It's fine to keep looking if you don't feel a connection or trust.

10. Cost and Insurance Analysis:

Understand the cost of therapy and determine whether the therapist accepts your insurance, if you have it. Discuss fees and payment choices if you're paying out of pocket.

11. Examine Ethics and Boundaries:

A competent therapist must adhere to strict ethical guidelines. Ascertain that the therapist follows ethical norms and maintains your anonymity.

12. Begin with a practice Session:

Consider starting with a few sessions to see if the therapist is a good fit for you. Before committing to long-term therapy, it's fine to try out several therapists.

13. Transparent Communication:

Open communication is the foundation of the therapeutic partnership. Feel free to speak with your therapist about your issues, goals, and expectations. Your feedback will help shape your therapy.

It is a personal adventure to find the proper therapist. It may take some time and searching, but once you discover a therapist with whom you connect, the potential for healing and personal growth is enormous. Remember that the ideal therapist is a collaborator on your path to better mental health and emotional well-being.

Support Groups and Communities

Individuals struggling with mental health issues, such as anxiety and phobias, might benefit from support groups and communities. These groups provide a sense of belonging, understanding, and shared experiences, thus establishing a secure and supportive environment for healing and growth. Let us look at the importance of support groups and communities in mental health.

1. Mutual Understanding:

Individuals who face similar issues are brought together by support groups and communities. Being in a group of individuals who understand your challenges, whether it's anxiety, specific phobias, or other mental health issues, can be really reassuring and validating.

2. Emotional Help:

Emotional support is one of the key roles of support groups. Members can share their emotions, worries, and anxieties honestly, knowing that they will be treated with respect and compassion. This emotional connection can help to ease feelings of loneliness and isolation.

3. Useful Information:

Members frequently share practical tips and coping tactics that have been effective for them. Learning from others' experiences might provide helpful insights into dealing with anxiety or phobias.

4. Experience Normalization:

Mental health issues can make people feel like outsiders. Anxiety and phobias are common and treatable disorders; thus, support groups help to normalize the experience. This normalization has the potential to lessen stigma and self-blame.

5. Disseminating Success Stories:

Members frequently share their success stories, demonstrating that recovery and growth are achievable. These stories provide hope and inspiration to those who are struggling.

6. Developing Coping Skills:

Coping skills training and education are typically included in support groups and communities. Members learn practical ways for managing symptoms and improving their mental health.

7. Accountability and Dedication:

Being a part of a supportive community might help you feel more accountable and committed. When members feel responsible to their group, they are more likely to attend treatment, practice self-help activities, and engage in self-care.

8. Isolation Reduction:

Isolation is a typical and severe side effect of mental health issues. Support groups reduce loneliness by providing a safe area for people to connect with others who understand and empathize with their problems.

9. Self-Expression Safe Zone:

Support groups and communities provide a safe and confidential environment in which individuals can freely express themselves without fear of judgements or stigmatization.

10. Diverse Points of View:

Support groups frequently include a diverse range of people with varying experiences and backgrounds. This variety can provide a more comprehensive perspective on mental health challenges and various coping mechanisms.

11. Online and Offline Options:

Online and in-person support groups and communities are available. Individuals can choose the format that is most comfortable and convenient for them because of this flexibility.

12. Peer Facilitators and Professional Counseling:

Some support groups are led by peers, and others are led by mental health professionals. Both approaches have advantages, as they provide a balance of shared experiences and expert counsel.

13. Ongoing Assistance:

Many support groups and communities provide ongoing assistance, allowing individuals to connect over time and receive ongoing encouragement.

Exploring support groups and communities can be a transforming step in your journey towards increased mental well-being, whether you're coping with anxiety, specific phobias, or any other mental health difficulty. The value of shared experiences, understanding, and support cannot be overstated, and these groups can be extremely beneficial to your healing and recovery.

Developing Healthy Habits for Efficient Anxiety Management

Anxiety is a frequent problem, but it can be effectively handled by adopting good behaviors and making lifestyle modifications. While anxiety management frequently entails therapy and, in some cases, medication, your everyday behaviors can help reduce anxiety symptoms and improve your general well-being. This post will look at good habits for anxiety management.

1. Consistent Exercise:

Physical activity serves as a natural stress reliever. Endorphins, or "feel-good" hormones, are released after exercise. Regular exercise can also help you sleep better and feel better in general.

2. Nutritional Balance:

A nutritious diet can have a favorable impact on your mental health. Caffeine and sweets should be avoided in excess because they might aggravate anxiety symptoms. Choose a diet high in fruits and vegetables, whole grains, lean proteins, and healthy fats.

3. Get Enough Sleep:

Sleep deprivation can exacerbate anxiety symptoms. Maintain a consistent sleep schedule and develop a peaceful bedtime routine to ensure you get enough rest.

4. Stress Management Methods:

Learn stress-reduction strategies such as deep breathing, progressive muscle relaxation, and mindfulness meditation as your role. These practices can assist you in remaining grounded and reducing worry.

5. Avoid Abuse of Alcohol and Other Substances:

Alcohol and other substances can aggravate anxiety symptoms. Reducing or discontinuing your usage of these substances can improve your mental health.

6. Reduce Screen Time:

Excessive screen usage, particularly on social media, can play a role in anxiety. Limit your screen time and engage in offline activities.

7. Time Administration:

The role of effective time management is to alleviate emotions of overburden and worry. Set reasonable goals, prioritize work, and divide larger tasks into smaller, manageable steps.

8. Create a Support System:

When you're feeling anxious or overwhelmed, having a support system of friends, family, or support groups can help you cope emotionally.

9. Cognitive Reorganization:

To confront unreasonable thoughts and beliefs, use cognitive restructuring. Change your thought processes to be more sensible and constructive.

10. Express Your Emotions:

Sharing your feelings with a trusted friend, family member, or therapist is your role. Talking about your worries can bring you relief and insight.

11. Make a Relaxation Area:

Designate a calm, quiet location to which you can retire when you need to rest and de-stress.

12. Participate in Creative Activities:

Art, writing, and music, for example, can be therapeutic and help you express your emotions.

13. Restrict Multitasking:

Instead of multitasking, focus on one task at a time. This can help to alleviate stress and anxiety.

14. Set attainable goals:

Avoid creating unrealistic expectations for yourself , as this can cause undue stress and anxiety.

15. Exercise Self-Compassion:

Be gentle and understanding with yourself. Recognize that setbacks and challenges are a normal part of the human experience. Treat yourself with the same kindness you would show a friend.

16. Seek Professional Assistance:

Seek professional help if your anxiety is severe or interferes with your daily life. Therapy and, in certain situations, medicines can be quite beneficial in the treatment of anxiety.

You can effectively manage anxiety and improve your mental well-being by implementing these healthy behaviors into your everyday routine. Remember that consistency is essential, and positive changes take time to show benefits. Be gentle with yourself as you develop these habits, and don't be afraid to seek further guidance and assistance from mental health specialists.

Diet and Exercise

Diet and exercise are important factors in anxiety management. Individuals can considerably lessen anxiety symptoms and improve their overall mental well-being by making wise eating choices and staying physically active. Let's look at how nutrition and exercise affect anxiety management.

Anxiety Management Diet:

1. Nutritional Balance:

A healthy diet rich in fruits, vegetables, whole grains, lean proteins, and healthy fats plays an important role in brain health. These meals can aid in mood regulation and anxiety reduction.

2. Fatty Acids Omega-3:

Omega-3 fatty acids, present in fatty fish (e.g. salmon, mackerel), flaxseeds, and walnuts have been demonstrated to improve mood and reduce anxiety.

3. Limit your intake of caffeine and sugar:

Caffeine and sugar consumption might aggravate anxiety symptoms. Reducing or eliminating these substances can aid in mood stabilization.

4. Hydration

The role of staying hydrated is critical for general wellness. Stress and anxiety can be exacerbated by dehydration.

5. Avoid Abuse of Alcohol and Other Substances:

Alcohol and other substances can exacerbate anxiety symptoms. Reducing or stopping their use may result in less anxiety.

6. Carbohydrates That are Complex:

Whole grains, for example, can help stabilize blood sugar levels and provide a constant release of energy, minimizing mood swings and anxiety.

7. Meals on a Regular Basis:

Consistent meal timing can help keep blood sugar levels stable. Skipping meals can cause anger and anxiety.

8. Digestive Health:

Emerging evidence indicates a link between gut health and mental wellness. Consuming probiotics and eating a diet that promotes gut health may reduce anxiety.

Anxiety Reduction Exercise:

1. Endorphin release:

Exercise causes the release of endorphins, which are natural mood elevators. Anxiety can be relieved by these "feel-good" chemicals.

2. Stress Management:

Regular physical activity is a good stress-reduction technique. It aids in the reduction of the body's stress reaction, making it simpler to deal with worry.

3. Improved Sleep:

Exercise enhances sleep quality, which is critical for anxiety management. A well-rested body and mind are less susceptible to stress.

4. Distraction and Concentration:

Physical activity can shift your attention away from worried thoughts, providing a mental respite from anxiety.

5. Interaction with Others:

Participating in group fitness activities can improve social contact, reduce feelings of isolation, and foster a sense of belonging, all of which can help with anxiety management.

6. Structure and Routine:

A regular exercise regimen can provide structure and consistency in your everyday life, which can be reassuring for people who suffer from anxiety.

7. Mind-Body Relationship:

Mindful exercises like yoga and tai chi improve the mind-body connection and relaxation, which helps to reduce anxiety symptoms.

8. Setting and Achieving Goals:

Setting and attaining fitness objectives can enhance self-esteem and self-confidence, which are important for anxiety management.

Putting Diet and Exercise Together

When nutrition and exercise are combined, a remarkable synergy is created. A nutritious diet offers the nutrients required for good physical and mental function, while exercise improves mood and decreases worry.

It's important to remember that the effects of food and exercise on anxiety control may not be immediate, and that consistency is critical. Consult a healthcare practitioner or a trained dietitian for personalized nutritional advice, and select an exercise routine that is appropriate for your interests and fitness level. A well-balanced diet combined with frequent physical activity can greatly help to reduce anxiety symptoms and improve general mental well-being.

Unlocking the Potential of Sleep and Stress Management

Sleep quality and stress management are critical components of mental health and well-being. These two pillars are critical in the treatment of anxiety and phobias. Let's look at the importance of sleep and stress management for Anxiety.

Anxiety Management with Quality Sleep:

1. Restored Sleep:

The role of quality sleep on cognitive functioning, emotional regulation, and overall well-being is critical. It allows the brain and body to rest and heal, and a lack of restorative sleep can exacerbate anxiety symptoms.

2. Reducing Anxiety:

Sleep has a significant impact on anxiety. Adequate sleep aids in mood regulation, irritation reduction, and anxiety reduction.

3. Anxiety Trigger Avoidance:

Role: Adequate sleep can help minimize common anxiety triggers such as exhaustion, mood swings, and cognitive deficits, all of which can increase anxiety symptoms.

4. Hygiene of Sleep:

Maintaining a consistent sleep schedule, adopting a tranquil nighttime routine, and optimizing your sleep surroundings all play a role in promoting quality sleep.

5. Avoidance of Stimulants:

Avoiding caffeine, nicotine, and big meals close to bedtime will help you fall asleep faster and sleep longer.

6. Stress Management:

Sleep is a natural stress reliever. Quality sleep aids in the recovery of the body from daily stressors and improves the ability to cope with stress.

Anxiety Stress Management that Works:

1. Meditation for Mindfulness:

Mindfulness plays a role. Meditation is a method that entails remaining totally present in the present moment. It aids in stress management by encouraging relaxation and self-awareness.

2. Exercises in Deep Breathing:

Deep breathing exercises can help folks feel more grounded and relaxed by reducing the body's stress reaction.

3. Muscle Relaxation in Stages:

This technique promotes physical and mental relaxation by systematically tensing and then relaxing different muscle groups.

4. Yoga:

Yoga is a practice that incorporates physical postures, breathing exercises, and meditation. It has the potential to relieve stress, increase flexibility, and promote general well-being.

5. Time Administration:

The role of effective time management is to reduce emotions of overburden and stress. Prioritizing work, setting attainable goals, and breaking major jobs down into smaller parts can all be beneficial.

6. Seeking Help:

Share your problems and thoughts with a trustworthy friend, family member, or therapist for emotional support and stress reduction.

7. Stress-Relieving Activities:

Spend time outdoors, listen to music, or engage in creative hobbies to relieve stress.

8. Problem-Solving Capabilities:

Develop problem-solving abilities to successfully address stress factors. Identifying potential answers and acting on them can be empowering and stress-reducing.

9. Professional Assistance:

If stress becomes overpowering or causes anxiety, consider obtaining professional assistance. Therapists can provide important stress management tools and approaches.

Combining Sleep and Stress Reduction:

Sleep and stress management are inextricably intertwined. Sleep deprivation can exacerbate stress, while prolonged stress can cause sleep difficulties. When efficient stress management is combined with enough sleep, a powerful synergy for anxiety reduction and overall mental wellness is created.

It takes time to develop healthy sleep habits and efficient stress management practices, and it's vital to remember that what works for one person may not work for another. Experiment with different ways and seek professional advice if necessary to find the combination that best matches your specific requirements and circumstances.

Anxiety and Phobia Management

A Holistic Approach

Holistic approaches to anxiety and phobia management take into account the whole person, concentrating on the mind, body, and spirit. These approaches Recognize the interdependence of mental health, physical well-being, emotional balance, and spiritual fulfillment . Let's look at holistic approaches to anxiety and phobia management.

1. Meditation and mindfulness:

Mindfulness and meditation approaches promote being in the moment, observing ideas without judgment, and attaining inner serenity. These techniques can help to reduce anxiety and increase emotional resilience.

2. Yoga:

Yoga is a practice that incorporates physical postures, breathing exercises, and meditation. It helps with anxiety management because it improves relaxation, flexibility, and emotional equilibrium.

3. Acupuncture:

Acupuncture is a traditional Chinese medicinal technique that involves inserting small needles into particular spots on the body. It can help you relax, reduce stress, and balance your energy flow.

4. Aromatherapy:

Aromatherapy utilizes essential oils to improve mental and emotional well-being. Certain smells, such as lavender and chamomile, are Recognized to be calming and anxiety-relieving.

5. Natural Supplements:

Some herbal supplements, such as valerian root and passionflower, are thought to have anxiety-relieving qualities. Before utilizing supplements, consult with a healthcare practitioner.

6. Nutritional Wellness:

Holistic diet takes into account the impact of food on mental and emotional wellness. A diet high in nutrient-dense, whole foods can improve mood and reduce anxiety.

7. Art Therapy and Creative Therapies:

Art therapy, music therapy, and other creative therapies allow people to express themselves creatively and relieve anxiety.

8. Healing with Energy:

Reiki and therapeutic touch, for example, involve balancing the body's energy to promote relaxation and emotional well-being.

9. Naturopathic Medicine (Naturopathic Medicine):

Naturopathic doctors manage anxiety with natural therapy and lifestyle changes. They may advise you to make dietary modifications, use herbal therapies, or take supplements.

10. Chiropractic Treatment:

Chiropractic therapy is concerned with the alignment of the spine and nerve system. Alignment can improve general health, including mental wellbeing.

11. Environmental Concerns:

A holistic approach may take into account the individual's environment, such as exposure to pollutants, natural light, and outdoor settings. A peaceful environment might be beneficial to one's mental health.

12. Movement and Exercise:

Physical activity is crucial for overall health and well-being. It alleviates anxiety, stimulates endorphin release, and promotes emotional balance.

13. Spiritual Link:

A spiritual connection can give comfort and resilience for certain people. Spiritual practices like prayer, meditation, or connecting with nature can improve one's emotional well-being.

14. Self-Care and Compassion:

The role of holistic approaches in mental health emphasizes self-compassion and self-care. Self-care and kindness to yourself can help alleviate anxiety and enhance well-being.

Holistic approaches Recognize that each person is unique, and that what works for one person may not work for another. These treatments frequently supplement established treatment methods and provide a well-rounded approach to anxiety and phobia management. It is critical to engage with healthcare professionals and holistic practitioners to develop a customized plan that matches your needs and is consistent with your beliefs and values.

CHAPTER 8

Building Resilience

DEVELOPING A MINDSET TO SURVIVE ADVERSITY

Developing a resilient attitude is essential for successfully managing anxiety and phobias, as well as addressing life's inevitable obstacles with strength and adaptation. Resilience is a skill that may be developed and polished over time rather than an inborn trait. , we will look at the essential principles and practices for cultivating a resilient attitude.

1. Accept Change as a Natural Process:

Resilient people understand that change is a natural and ongoing element of life. Instead of being afraid of it, they see it as a chance for progress.

2. Develop a Positive Self-Image:

A resilient attitude is characterized by a positive self-perception. Develop self-compassion, self-acceptance, and an emphasis on your strengths.

3. Increase Emotional Awareness:

Understanding your emotions and how they affect your ideas and behaviors is your role. Emotional awareness enables you to respond more effectively to difficult situations.

4. Improve Problem-Solving Skills:

The role of resilience is to find solutions to difficulties. Improve your problem-solving abilities to deal with problems in a proactive manner.

5. Exercise Adaptability:

Individuals that are resilient are adaptable and receptive to new techniques and viewpoints. You can adjust to shifting conditions if you are flexible.

6. Create a Support Network:

The importance of having a robust support network cannot be overstated. Surround yourself with individuals who will encourage, empathize, and understand you.

7. Adversity teaches us:

Adversity should be viewed as an opportunity for personal progress. Reflect on adversities to develop wisdom and understanding.

8. Establish Realistic Goals:

The role of resilience is to set attainable goals that are adaptive to changing conditions. Setting reasonable goals gives a sense of accomplishment.

9. Create a Sense of Purpose:

A strong feeling of purpose and meaning in one's life can boost resilience. It motivates people to overcome obstacles.

10. Maintain Physical Fitness:

Physical well-being and mental resilience are connected. Regular exercise, a healthy diet, and enough sleep all contribute to overall resilience.

11. Practice Mindfulness and Relaxation Techniques:

Mindfulness and relaxation techniques help reduce stress and enhance emotional equilibrium, both of which are necessary for resilience.

12. Seek Professional Assistance:

Seek expert assistance whenever necessary. Therapists and counselors can offer helpful advice and tactics for developing resilience.

13. Reframing Negative Thoughts:

Resilient people rephrase negative beliefs into more positive ones. Replacing illogical ideas with rational and empowering perspectives.

14. Accept Imperfections:

Accept the idea that perfection is unattainable. Recognizing that mistakes and failures are part of the human experience is essential for resilience.

15. Keep a Sense of Humor:

Humor can be an effective coping tool. It enables you to chuckle even in adverse conditions.

16. Develop Gratitude:

The role of thankfulness in boosting resilience is that it fosters a positive outlook and a sense of abundance.

17. Study Role Models:

Identify and learn from resilient people who inspire you. Their experiences might provide inspiration and insight.

Creating a resilient mindset is a continuous process that requires self-awareness, self-care, and a desire to learn from life's adversities. With time and practice, you may develop resilience that will not only help you manage anxiety and phobias, but will also allow you to thrive in the face of adversity.

Setting Realistic Goals for Anxiety and Phobia Management

Setting realistic goals is an important part of successfully treating anxiety and phobias. Realistic goals create a clear path for advancement, encourage action, and deliver a sense of accomplishment. Let's look at why it's important to set realistic goals and how to do it effectively.

Why Establish Realistic Goals:

Setting realistic goals gives your efforts a defined direction. They assist you in focusing on specific goals, making your path to overcome anxiety and phobias more bearable. Motivation can be increased by setting small, attainable goals. Each achievement strengthens your belief in your ability to conquer obstacles. It also helps you monitor your progress. This allows you to evaluate what is working and, if necessary, alter your approach. Overwhelm can be avoided by breaking down huge projects into smaller, more manageable steps. It makes the process easier to handle.

Setting Realistic Goals:

Determine Specific Objectives:

Define your objectives precisely. Rather than a general objective like "reduce anxiety," set a specific goal like "practice deep breathing exercises for 10 minutes every day."

Make Your Objectives Measurable:

Make sure you can track your progress. For example, if your objective is to attend social gatherings without feeling anxious, you can log how many social events you attend and how you feel during each one.

Ensure that Your Objectives are Attainable:

Think about your current abilities and resources. Set goals that are difficult yet doable with effort. Unrealistic ambitions can be discouraging.

Relevance:

Make certain that your goals are relevant to your general well-being as well as the specific issues you confront. Goals that are relevant to you are more likely to motivate you.

Timetables Must Be Established:

Determine a fair timetable for reaching your objectives. For example, you could set a goal to "reduce panic attack frequency by 50% within three months."

Break Down Larger Objectives:

If you have a large objective, divide it into smaller, more manageable tasks. If your main goal is to "speak in public without excessive fear," a minor step could be to "enroll in a public speaking course."

Be adaptable:

Life is unpredictable, and growth does not always follow a straight route. Be adaptable and willing to change your goals as needed.

Seek Professional Help:

Consult with a mental health expert or therapist to assist you in setting and refining your goals. They can offer experienced advice and assistance.

Realistic Goals for Anxiety and Phobia Management:

Deep breathing exercises should be done for 10 minutes every day to lessen anxiety symptoms. Attend one social event per month with a friend to progressively conquer social phobia.

In phobia treatment, gradually increase exposure to the feared object or circumstance by attending a series of structured exposure sessions. Keep a daily anxiety journal to keep track of triggers and symptoms and to spot patterns. Consult a therapist to learn and practice cognitive-behavioral approaches for effectively managing anxiety and phobias.

Remember that the road to anxiety and phobia management is a personal one, and your goals should reflect your own needs and circumstances. Realistic goals serve as a road map for your progress, providing a sense of direction and success as you work towards a life free of anxiety and phobia-related issues.

Overcoming Difficulties in Anxiety and Phobia Management Through Resilience

Setbacks are a natural part of any journey, and they are to be expected when dealing with anxiety and phobias. The goal is to understand how to deal with setbacks rather than avoid them. Let's look at ways to deal with setbacks in anxiety and phobia control in this article.

1. View setbacks as learning experiences:

Instead of seeing setbacks as failures, consider them to be opportunities for growth and learning. Examine what went wrong and what you can do better next time.

2. Exercise Self-Compassion:

When you face difficulties, be gentle and compassionate to yourself. Self-criticism can be harmful and lead to greater anxiety. Treat yourself with the same compassion that you would extend to a friend.

3. Keep Things in Perspective:

Remind yourself that setbacks are just temporary. They do not represent your total progress. Keep your long-term objectives in mind and concentrate on the broader picture.

4. Seek Outside Help:

When you suffer setbacks, don't be afraid to seek help from friends, family, or a therapist. Speaking with someone you can trust can give you emotional comfort as well as helpful insights.

5. Adapt and Modify:

Setbacks may necessitate a shift in strategy. To handle the obstacles you have, modify your approach and consider attempting new solutions.

6. Set Resilience-Building Techniques into Action:

When faced with setbacks, mindfulness, relaxation exercises, and other resilience-building strategies can help you stay grounded and manage stress.

7. Maintain Your Commitment to Your Goals:

Setbacks can be discouraging, but it's critical to stick to your long-term goals. Remind yourself why you chose this path in the first place.

8. Use Setbacks as a Guideline:

Use setbacks as a yardstick for measuring your development. They can assist you in identifying areas for improvement and provide essential input.

9. Divide Your Goals Into Smaller Steps:

Sometimes setbacks occur as a result of overly ambitious initial goals. To reduce the possibility of setbacks, divide your goals into smaller, more manageable tasks.

10. Recognize Small Victories:

Recognize and celebrate minor accomplishments along the road. These can help you feel more motivated and accomplished.

11. Control Expectations:

Set reasonable expectations for your adventure. Accept that setbacks are a normal part of the process and do not represent your value.

12. Seek Professional Assistance:

Consider consulting with a mental health professional if setbacks are very difficult and impede your progress. They can offer advice and custom tactics.

Dealing with setbacks is an important skill in anxiety and phobia management. You can overcome problems and continue your journey towards a life with less anxiety and phobia-related difficulties by perceiving setbacks as chances for growth, practicing self-compassion, and remaining devoted to your goals. Remember that encountering and overcoming setbacks builds resilience, making you stronger in the long term.

CONCLUSION

Building A Life Of Well-being And Fulfillment Beyond Anxiety And Phobias

Thriving with anxiety and phobias is about establishing a life filled with well-being, purpose, and fulfillment , not just managing symptoms. Let's look at tactics and approaches to help you not just overcome anxiety and phobias but also thrive in many facets of your life.

1. Establish Your Values and Goals:

Begin by identifying your principles and establishing relevant life goals. Understanding what is most important to you can give you a sense of purpose and direction.

2. Make self-care a priority:

Self-care is critical for general well-being. Include self-care practices in your everyday routine, such as activities that promote your physical, emotional, and mental wellbeing.

3. Develop Resilience:

Resilience is the ability to recover from misfortune. Practice adaptive coping skills, set realistic objectives, and learn from setbacks to build resilience.

4. Keep a Support System:

Surround yourself with a network of friends, family, or support groups who can offer emotional support and understanding.

5. Continue Your Education:

The role of knowledge is to empower. Continue to learn about anxiety, phobias, and self-improvement tactics. Education can help you understand these issues and equip you with the tools you need to deal with them.

6. Push Yourself Outside of Your Comfort Zone:

Challenge your comfort zone gradually by confronting your worries and anxieties. Exposure therapy and cognitive-behavioral approaches can assist you in becoming desensitized to phobic triggers.

7. Recognize Achievements:

Recognize and appreciate your accomplishments, no matter how big or small. Recognizing your accomplishments can increase your self-esteem and motivation.

8. Practice Mindful Activities:

Mindfulness meditation and relaxation techniques can assist you in remaining present and reducing stress. These techniques improve your emotional well-being and ability to deal with anxiety.

9. Emphasize Your Strengths:

Change your focus from your weaknesses to your strengths. Identify your distinct abilities and apply them to your personal and professional lives.

10. Volunteer:

Helping others or contributing to a greater good can bring a sense of purpose and fulfillment .

11. Seek Professional Help:

Consult with a mental health practitioner or therapist if necessary to treat specific anxiety or phobia-related issues. They can provide specialized advice and assistance.

12. Keep Relapse Prevention in Mind:

Even after making a significant recovery, keep an eye out for future relapses. Create ways to avoid setbacks and maintain your health.

13. Follow your interests and passions:

Hobbies and interests that bring you joy and fulfillment can be a great way to thrive in the face of worry and phobias.

14. Strive for Work-Life Balance:

A balance between your business and personal lives is critical for your well-being. Make time for relaxation, recreation, and quality time with loved ones.

15. Accept Flexibility:

Life is dynamic, and sometimes adaptability is essential. Accept change and adapt to new situations while remaining true to your principles and ambitions.

Thriving with Anxiety and Phobias is a journey of personal development, resilience, and self-discovery. It is about living a life that corresponds with your values, fulfills your passions, and gives you a sense of well-being and fulfillment. By incorporating these methods and practices into your life, you can begin to thrive rather than just manage your anxiety and phobias.

Mental Health Support Helplines And Hotlines

Individuals in need of emergency mental health support, crisis intervention, or information can benefit from helplines and hotlines. They provide a lifeline to people suffering from emotional anguish, anxiety, phobias, and other mental health issues. Let's look at some of the helplines and hotlines that can aid you or someone you know in times of need:

Lifeline for Suicide Prevention:

This lifeline provides 24-hour care to people in distress, especially those who are suicidal. Counselors are trained to provide confidential support and resources.

Phone: 1-800-273-8255

Text Line for Emergencies:

The Crisis Text Line is open 24 hours a day, seven days a week. Text with certified crisis counselors who can offer emotional support and assist you in navigating challenging situations. Text "HELLO" to 741741.

SAMHSA (Substance Abuse and Mental Health Services Administration) National Helpline:

The SAMHSA helpline provides free, confidential support to anyone suffering from mental health and substance use disorders. They can assist you in locating local treatment alternatives and resources. Call 1-800-662-HELP (4357)

Helpline for the National Alliance on Mental Illness (NAMI):

NAMI's HelpLine serves individuals and families affected by mental health issues with information, resources, and support. Trained volunteers provide direction and help.
Call 1-800-950-NAMI (6264).

Trevor's Project:

The Trevor Project assists LGBTQ+ kids in crisis, especially those suffering from anxiety, depression, and suicidal ideation. They give a safe, confidential environment for people to talk.
Phone: 1-866-488-7386
Send a text message with the word "TREVOR" to 1-202-304-1200.

Crisis Line for Veterans:

This lifeline gives assistance to veterans and their families. Individuals experiencing mental distress or suicidal ideation are assisted by trained responders.

Call 1-800-273-8255 and press 1.

"838255" is a text message.

The Trans Lifeline:

Trans Lifeline's role is to provide crisis support to transgender and non-binary people. They offer discreet support for emotional discomfort and related issues.

Phone: 1-877-565-8860

Helpline for Disasters:

The Disaster Distress Helpline provides crisis support to people facing emotional distress as a result of disasters, such as natural disasters and public health situations.

Phone: 1-800-985-5990

Helpline for the National Eating Disorders Association (NEDA):

The NEDA's helpline provides support and information to people suffering from eating disorders, which are frequently accompanied by anxiety and sadness.

Phone: 1-800-931-2237

Childhelp International's National Child Abuse Hotline:

The purpose of this hotline is to prevent and treat child abuse. It offers assistance and services to children and families who are facing difficult circumstances.

Contact us at 1-800-4-A-CHILD (1-800-422-4453).

These hotlines and helplines offer instant aid, crisis intervention, and emotional support. If you or someone you know is experiencing mental health issues, please do not hesitate to call out to these resources. Consider obtaining continuous care and therapy from mental health specialists and therapists as well.

JOURNAL